Contents

4
2

Social Work Practice with Older Lesbians and Gay Men

Social Work Practice with Older Lesbians and Gay Men

LEE-ANN FENGE
ANN FANNIN
CHRISTINA HICKS
NICHOLA LAVIN

Series Editor: **Keith Brown**

LearningMatters

First published in 2008 by Learning Matters Ltd

British Library Cataloguing in Publication Data
A CIP record for this book is available from the British Library.

ISBN 978 1 84445 182 1

Cover design by Code 5 Design Associates Ltd
Project management by Deer Park Productions
Typeset by Pantek Arts Ltd, Maidstone, Kent
Printed and bound in Great Britain by Bell & Bain Ltd, Glasgow

Learning Matters Ltd
33 Southernhay East
Exeter EX1 1NX
Tel: 01392 215560
info@learningmatters.co.uk
www.learningmatters.co.uk

QUESTIONNAIRE

As an introduction to our text, we have compiled an awareness questionnaire for people to test their knowledge of the issues concerning older homosexual people.

This questionnaire is about awareness and knowledge and not about seeking to prove prejudice or discrimination. It is hoped that those who are new to the issues of older lesbian and gay people will start by looking at the questions to alert them to the topic. Some questions may have no clear answers; to others it is possible to answer Yes or No. However, all have a potential for discussion and debate. They are here to get the thinking processes started. At the end of the book (pages 85–6) we shall seek to clarify the themes.

The term 'older' is understood, in this instance, to refer to people over 55.

Questionnaire

1. How many older lesbians, gay men or bisexual people do you think you have met?

2. Do you know what percentage of older people are gay?

3. If you work/ed as a carer with older people, either in their own homes, residential care or in a sheltered housing unit, would you 'treat everyone the same'?

4. How do you understand the term 'equal opportunities'?

5. Do you think older gay people have different care needs from those who are heterosexual?

6. Can you recognise a lesbian, a gay man or a bisexual person?

7. If a person has children and grandchildren, does this mean they cannot possibly be gay?

8. Many lesbians and gay men want to have care services specifically for gay people; why do you think this is?

9. What do you understand by the terms 'institutional homophobia' and 'internalised homophobia'?

10. Do you believe that sexual orientation is a 'private matter' and no one else's business?

Background and introduction

By Keith Brown and Lee-Ann Fenge

This text has been written to provide a deeper understanding of the diversity within the ageing population, and specifically the needs and experiences of older lesbians and gay men, and the implications for social work practice. It provides knowledge and guidance for practitioners, managers and social work students alike. It is written as a series of self-contained chapters to support learning and practice development, and contributors include older volunteer researchers involved in a recent research project, the project worker who supported the volunteers during the project, as well as ourselves. As such, it is a collaborative effort and one that not only values the practitioner and academic perspective, but has at its centre the perspectives of older lesbians and gay men themselves.

Although specifically written for social workers undertaking a Post Qualifying Social Work award, it is of great value to all professionals who work with older people. The voice and experience of older lesbians and gay men can be clearly heard in this text and, importantly, issues relating to the practice of professionals with this sector of the population are drawn out.

The messages from the various contributors to this text have not been altered or influenced in any way by the two of us. We have been conscious of how often professionals and academics can 'filter' the voice of the service user, carer or client. We have striven hard not to do this. We have simply helped to facilitate the contributors by providing encouragement and a vehicle for them to write down their views and experiences. We hope that you will agree with us that their contributions are of great value to practitioners working with this client group. Indeed, one of our personal reflections has been how little is written about this area of practice coupled with how much insight, analysis and practical advice our fellow contributors have brought to this text.

Personally and professionally it has been a great privilege and opportunity for us to be involved with this research and this text. We sincerely hope and trust you will find it of great value in your professional practice.

This text should help you with your professional role in meeting the following national occupational standards for social work.

Key Role 1:   Prepare for and work with individuals, families, carers, groups and communities to assess their needs and circumstances

   2.2   Work with individuals, families, carers, groups and communities to identify, gather, analyse and understand information

2.3 Work with individuals, families, carers, groups and communities to enable them to analyse, identify, clarify and express their strengths, expectations and limitations

2.4 Work with individuals, families, carers, groups and communities to enable them to assess and make informed decisions about their needs, circumstances, risks, preferred options and resources

3.1 Assess and review the preferred options of individuals, families, carers, groups and communities

Key Role 2: Plan, carry out, review and evaluate social work practice, with individuals, families, carers, groups, communities and other professionals

5.1 Develop and maintain relationships with individuals, families, carers, groups, communities and others

7.1 Examine with individuals, families, carers, groups, communities and others support networks which can be accessed and developed

7.2 Work with individuals, families, carers, groups, communities and others to initiate and sustain support networks

Key Role 3: Support individuals to represent their needs, views and circumstances

10.1 Assess whether you should act as an advocate for the individual, family, carer, group or community

10.2 Assist individuals, families, carers, groups and communities to access independent advocacy

10.3 Advocate for, and with, individuals, families, carers, groups and communities

Key Role 6: Demonstrate professional competence in social work practice

18.1 Review and update your own knowledge of legal, policy and procedural frameworks

18.2 Use professional and organisational supervision and support to research, critically analyse and review knowledge-based practice

18.3 Implement knowledge-based social work models and methods to develop and improve your own practice

19.3 Work within the principles and values underpinning social work practice

21.1 Contribute to policy review and development

21.2 Use supervision and organisational and professional systems to inform a course of action where practice falls below required standards

21.3 Work with colleagues to contribute to team development

Throughout this book you will notice that occasionally the term 'gay' is used generically to encompass lesbians, gay men and bisexuals. This could be deemed controversial. From the early 1970s many radical lesbians have felt it important to keep a distinct identity from gay men. While recognising the legitimacy of this debate, it can be less cumbersome to use a generic term. Words tend to change emphasis over time and it has become much more acceptable within lesbian circles to describe themselves as gay women – indeed, some now prefer to. It is believed the word 'gay' originated from the liberation marches of the 1970s where one of the most popular slogans was 'Good As You'. These marches were made up of both male and female homosexual people.

Although it is accepted that most of the issues that affect lesbian and gay people also affect bisexual and transgender people, the research that informed this book was looking specifically at the needs and experiences of older lesbians and gay men. This is a complex area of debate and one that is not explored in these chapters. Nonetheless, reference to lesbian and gay (LG) issues within the text could also be relevant for lesbian, gay, bisexual and transsexual people (LGBT).

Keith Brown holds professional qualifications in nursing and social work, and teaching and academic qualifications in nursing, social work and management. He has worked in education and training for more than 20 years for universities and local authority social work departments and is currently the Director of the Centre for Post Qualifying Social Work at Bournemouth University. He is the series editor for the Learning Matters Post Qualifying Social Work series of textbooks. In 2005, he was awarded the Linda Ammon Memorial Prize sponsored by the Department for Education and Skills, awarded to the individual making the greatest contribution to education and training in the UK. The Centre for Post Qualifying Social Work was also awarded the Chartered Institute for Personnel and Development Prize for the Best Example of a Continuous Professional Development programme in the UK.

Ann Fannin has been involved in the Gay and Grey research project from the outset and is keen to further the cause of older lesbians and gay men in the future. She has been a life-long campaigner for peace and justice in many spheres and is a committed socialist. Much of her working life has been spent in social services with older people. She has three adult children and two grandchildren, all of whom she adores. She lives with her partner Joyce in the heart of the New Forest and has a passion for horses. One of her favourite (African) proverbs is 'You think you're too small to make a difference? Then you've obviously never slept in the same room as a mosquito'.

Lee-Ann Fenge practised as a social worker in a number of settings in adult social services, both in London and Dorset, before joining Bournemouth University as a lecturer in 1995. Her particular interests are in practice with older people and community care, and she teaches on the BA (Hons) Vulnerable Adults/Community Care degree at Bournemouth University. Alongside the Gay and Grey research project she also developed and taught a research programme for older people in Community Survey Research, funded by Older and Bolder, in September 2004. She is currently completing doctoral work on widening participation and the role of foundation degrees.

Christina Hicks has had a varied career including the armed forces (from which she was discharged for her sexuality) and the National Health Service, as well as being a qualified funeral director. She has considerable experience of carrying out both large and small health-related surveys and writing the associated reports. Since retiring from full-time employment she has carried out assessments on voluntary groups applying for charitable funding, participated in the development of a social group for lesbians and continued her love of theatre in addition to numerous other community activities.

Nichola Lavin was employed by Help and Care as the facilitator for Gay and Grey for the first 18 months of the project. She found this a challenging, enjoyable and very rewarding role. Prior to this she worked for Connexions, providing advice and guidance to young people across Dorset. She left the project in order to move nearer to her family in Birmingham, where she is now undertaking a degree in social work.

Chapter 1

Developing inclusive practice: background to the Gay and Grey project

By Lee-Ann Fenge

This text has grown out of a research project called 'Gay and Grey in Dorset', which took place between 2003 and 2006 and culminated in the publication of the 'Lifting the lid' report in 2006. This research project came about as a joint initiative between Bournemouth University and Help and Care, a voluntary agency working with older people and their carers in Dorset. In 2000, I approached Help and Care in the hope of developing possible joint research initiatives exploring the needs of older people in the local community. My previous practice background had been in both hospital and area social work teams working with older people, and developing practice with older people had continued to be a focus of my work at Bournemouth University.

It was felt that a project exploring the needs of minority groups of older people in the local community would be a worthwhile area to research and, based on local demographics, it was decided to focus the study on the needs of older lesbians and gay men. This was an opportune time to develop this research project as Age Concern was just raising the profile of the needs of older lesbians and gay men nationally through its publication *Opening doors* (2001) and government policy was highlighting the diversity of experience within the ageing population.

Until recently in the United Kingdom, little effort had been made to consider the needs and experiences of older lesbians and gay men (OLGs), and this area has remained largely unexplored in social policy and social work. This has meant that older members of the gay community have been invisible (Heaphy et al., 2004) and have failed to be considered in terms of their social and health care needs.

The Gay and Grey project 2003–06

The aim of the Gay and Grey project was to explore and understand better the experiences of older lesbians and gay men in Bournemouth, Poole and Dorset and used a participatory action research (PAR) model (Heron, 1996). This methodology was chosen because neither I as lead researcher nor the co-ordinator within Help and Care were either lesbian or older. We did not want to impose our 'outsider' perspectives on the project and therefore we engaged in an early pilot project with the local older lesbian and gay communities before we applied for research funding. Firstly this was to ensure that the local communities would be interested in the project, and secondly it was to ensure that volunteers would be involved from the outset of the project. Following the initial pilot project, an application was made to the Big Lottery Fund. Following an initial rejection and resubmission, funding was eventually confirmed in April 2003 for a three-year project.

A participatory research process meant that the volunteers could 'own' the research and be central in undertaking the research project themselves. It is informed by critical social theory, which identifies inequalities within traditional relationships between researchers and participants. It therefore represents a paradigm shift in the traditional role of researcher and subjects. Research which is directed and undertaken by service users or volunteers contests the nature and control of knowledge and 'necessitates reframing the social relations of research sponsorship and production, shifting the balance of power away from the professional' (Ross et al., 2005, p.267). It therefore recognises the expertise of volunteers, enabling them to share their own experiences and 'insider' knowledge. This approach sat comfortably with the ethos of Help and Care as an organisation and with my own personal stance towards research which would empower rather than disempower those involved. Our choice of approach was facilitated by reference to Arnstein's (1971) ladder of citizen participation which outlines a continuum of participation from manipulation (non-participation) to citizen control (citizen power), (Figure 1).

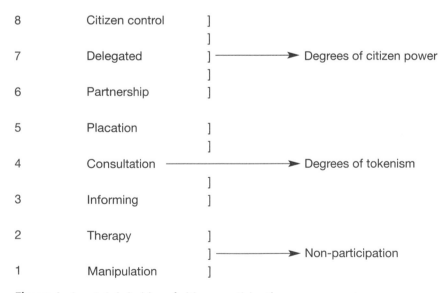

Figure 1 *Arnstein's ladder of citizen participation*

We hoped that our research would have a high level of citizen power in terms of the project being driven by the volunteers and the research project being undertaken by the volunteers with our support.

The potential empowering nature of involving service users and volunteers in research has also been highlighted by Hanley et al. (2004), who suggest that 'involvement in research often provides a route to change and improvement in issues which concern people most' (p.4). Hanley et al. (2004) suggest a simplified model of Arnstein's work which offers a continuum of involvement with three levels of service user/volunteer involvement in research (Figure 2).

CONSULTATION ⎯⎯⎯⎯⎯⎯▶ COLLABORATION ⎯⎯⎯⎯⎯⎯▶ USER CONTROL

Figure 2 *Hanley's continuum of involvement*

Increasingly, service users and citizens in general are expected to take on a greater role in the evaluation and development of public services and as such are becoming increasingly involved in consultations about service delivery and quality (Gilliatt et al., 2000).

Consultation can be seen as asking people about their views on a particular issue, possibly at a one-off event such as a meeting where views are being sought on a particular policy or approach. Collaboration may be seen as a more active, ongoing partnership with members of the public who may join a steering group or committee. User control involvement usually signifies that the locus of power is with the service users/volunteers. However, it does not necessarily mean that they undertake every stage of the research or that the professional researcher is totally excluded.

I believe that the Gay and Grey project sat at the 'user control' end of the continuum because all aspects of the project were undertaken by the volunteers, although I and the project worker were involved in supporting them through the process and were not excluded from it. For example, a small group of four volunteers undertook 30 in-depth interviews and the subsequent analysis of the data. I joined the group in the analysis stage and offered support throughout the data analysis and write-up. However, I perceived my role as a 'support' rather than as a 'lead'. As Hanley et al. (2004) conclude, 'user-controlled research might broadly be interpreted as research where the locus of power, initiative and subsequent decision making is with service users rather than professional researchers' (p.10).

ACTIVITY 1

Using Hanley et al.'s (2004) involvement continuum, consider the ways in which your organisation works with service users and/or volunteers in research and practice development activities.

Acknowledging the voices of service users and volunteers – the power of the pen

The development of this textbook has reinforced further the contributions that 'non-professionals' such as service users and volunteers can make to social work knowledge and practice development. The majority of the chapters have been written by the older volunteers involved in the project who have also been key in deciding on the focus and scope of the text. This embraces the notion of empowering practice and user involvement as being central tenets of social work. It is not enough just to ask service users/carers/volunteers for their views, but they need to become central players within social work research, practice development and education.

For some time there has been an awareness within social work practice of seeing people as 'experts' in their own lives, and to work in ways which empower rather than disempower (Smale et al., 2000). At the same time, the government has acknowledged the central role that service users and carers have in the design and delivery of social work education (Department of Health, 2002). However, the labels 'service user', 'carer' and 'volunteer' can have a disempowering effect in terms of preserving the *status quo* of 'professional' and 'non-professional'. Although the government rhetoric raises the profile of the contributions of service users to the design and delivery of social work education, the label may work against this process 'if those that it refers to and those that use it see it as stigmatising' (Hefferman, 2006, p.826). It is therefore important for practitioners to be aware of the power of language and terminology, and the potentially disempowering impact it can have. As Bourdieu (1997) suggests, those in power have a means of using language as a way to preserve their domination.

As social workers and social work educators, we need to contest dominant discourses and practices concerning minority groups and assist them to develop new knowledge and truths about their lives and experiences. The experiences of 'minority' groups can be lost by the imposing assumptions and dominant cultural processes (Lupnitz, 1992). Research methods which serve to reinforce the power of the researcher over the power of the participants may support rather than challenge professional knowledge. As Foucault (1980) suggests, knowledge and power are inseparable. It is therefore vital to appreciate the oppressive nature of current professional knowledge and the opportunity to empower oppressed groups through the development of new knowledge (Hartman, 1992). A participatory action research (PAR) methodology goes some way to redress this imbalance and enables minority groups to define and contribute to knowledge and understanding about their lives.

Yet there is a paradox in this methodological approach. Pure PAR could be described as 'ground up' in the sense that the impetus for the research comes from the community itself. However, in this project, both Help and Care and I held some power in the research process as initiators of the idea and the ones who secured funding to take the project forward. This paradox has been described by Healy (2001), who identifies the power of researchers as both initiators of research and promoters of participant involvement. It was important, therefore, to remain reflective and vigilant throughout the research process, acknowledging how personal stance and power can exert an influence on research participants and volunteers (Savin-Baden, 2004).

It is perhaps also useful to view participatory research as a continuum (Heron, 1996) where one pole is community-controlled processes and the other is researcher-controlled processes (Figure 3). This project sits most comfortably somewhere in the middle, with the initial idea and ongoing support from a researcher but with volunteers 'owning' the research process by steering the project, undertaking the research, analysing findings and disseminating the results. The volunteers were also central in raising the profile of the project with local health, housing and social care providers by undertaking outreach visits and joining local groups. I was constantly amazed by the boundless energy and enthusiasm that the volunteers brought to the project, but I feel on reflection that this was because they all felt so passionate about and committed to challenging current practice with older lesbians and gay men, and ultimately promoting acceptance of diversity within the ageing population.

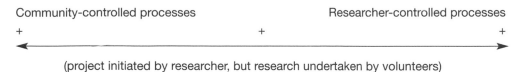

(project initiated by researcher, but research undertaken by volunteers)

Figure 3 *Participatory research continuum*

The project was undertaken 'with' people rather than 'on' people. This method is particularly valuable when working with groups who have experienced discrimination and oppression as it values their cultural experiences and enables participants to give voice to their own perspectives and beliefs (Troyna and Carrington, 1989). It therefore offers an 'insider' perspective that comes 'from inside the culture, from the premises of the people and their situation' (Swantz, 1996, p.124).

Despite the paradox that 'outsiders' do have power and roles to play within PAR projects, it is important to recognise that participatory action research is an 'emancipatory' model. The volunteers used transferable skills from previous careers and life experiences, as well as developing new skills particularly related to research methods and data analysis. They 'owned' the project and from the start the volunteers 'led' the process with the support of the project worker and university-based researcher. Since the end of the funded project in November 2006, a number of volunteers have remained engaged with the aims of the project, which included the need to disseminate the findings and develop education and training resources for practitioners.

Supporting service users and volunteers to write about their experiences and perspectives is a central part of developing new knowledge in social work. The contributions in this text are the volunteers' own words and opinions. They have not been filtered by me or the editor of the text. During the research project I was constantly aware of maintaining a stance that would enable me to support the volunteers as they requested, but not in a way that filtered or changed the outputs of the project. Similarly, as this textbook developed, I was mindful to support the volunteers in writing their own chapters, providing support with references and materials as requested, but being sure that the volunteers were encouraged to write their contributions as they wished to. This highlights the importance of being vigilant to the ways in which filters operate to block or alter the perspectives of services users and/or volunteers in social work research and practice development. The language used and the meanings that are attached to the words of service users and/or volunteers may be misinterpreted or filtered and as a result the essence may be lost.

However, it is also important to remember that the voices emerging from the research, and indeed the contributors within this text, do not represent the experiences and views of all older lesbian and gay people. We therefore do not assume homogeneity among the older lesbian and gay population.

This project took place at a time when there was increased awareness from government about the social exclusion of certain groups within society, and this is demonstrated by the formation of the Social Exclusion Unit (Cabinet Office, 2001). Growing awareness of the impact of discrimination and exclusion on older people's lives has also led to policy initiatives such as the National Service Framework for Older People, which highlights rooting out age discrimination within Standard One (Department of Health, 2001), and policies from the Audit Commission (2004) which seek inclusion of older people rather than exclusion.

The Audit Commission report promotes the involvement of older people as central partners in initiatives that affect the lives of older people. At the same time, there is increased interest in the participation of older people within the communities in which they live, as well as wider participation in the form of political activity (Postle et al., 2005). One of the key themes of New Labour's modernisation agenda has been to put service users, carers and volunteers at the heart of social care (Department of Health, 1998, 2000).

ACTIVITY 2

Think of the ways in which your practice setting promotes the involvement of older people as partners in initiatives that affect their lives. How meaningful is this involvement? Do older service users/carers/participants have a real voice in matters that impact on their lives?

The Gay and Grey project's participative methodology fits comfortably with an 'inclusive' approach because it used a participatory model of research and allowed the often hidden voices of a minority group to be heard. However, even within participatory models of involvement, it is important to be aware of and question whose voices are actually being heard and how representative they are of the wider group. This is particularly important when working with 'hidden' populations, such as older lesbians and gay men, where some individuals may wish to remain hidden and so their particular voices and experiences will not be heard.

A number of key priorities was identified by the research including:

- the development of awareness training programmes to counteract homophobic prejudice and the assumption of heterosexuality
- anti-discriminatory policies allowing for diversity and equality enshrined in codes of practice for everyone who works with older people
- lesbian and gay-friendly services (including bereavement counselling, buddying schemes, gay-friendly advocacy and home support).

(Gay and Grey in Dorset, 2006, p.83)

One of the key themes identified by this project was the need to develop awareness training about the lives and experiences of older lesbians and gay men within the health and social care workforce, and to promote an understanding of the wide diversity within the ageing population of the UK. This textbook therefore forms part of an ongoing commitment from the volunteers to disseminate their findings and to promote an increased awareness among staff who work with older people of the great diversity within the ageing population.

The book has been structured around key themes that emerged during the project and is co-written by a number of volunteers, as well as university staff and the project worker. However, in this chapter I will briefly explore the background of ageism and discrimination that affects all older people so as to provide a backdrop to the other chapters. Factors such as sexuality, gender, ethnicity, disability and class will significantly impact upon how ageing is experienced and managed, and are central to our understanding of how individuals and groups become marginalised and socially excluded within society.

Ageism, discrimination and social exclusion

In Britain we live within a culture which has tended to value 'youth' while devaluing age and ageing. Images of older people are often invisible in the media, and where they are present, they tend to depict unattractive, confused, physically frail and emotionally isolated individuals (Barnett, 2006). Research into lesbian and gay lifestyles has tended to replicate this pattern, being predominantly concerned with youthful experience (Heaphy et al., 2004).

Ageism closes people's minds to older people, making them invisible to society. It has been described as 'a systematic stereotyping of and discrimination against older people because they are old' (Butler, 1989, p.139). Others have identified both positive and negative attributes associated with ageism as the following definition by Schaie (1993) illustrates:

> *Ageism may be defined as a form of culturally based age bias that involves (a) restrictiveness of behaviour or opportunities based on age, age-based stereo-typing, and distorted perception in the service of maintaining such stereotypes, positive or negative; (b) a cultural belief that age is a significant dimension by definition and that it defines a person's social position, psychological characteristics or individual experience.* (p.49)

Age is used to stigmatise individuals and to characterise them as problematic and this is reinforced by models of ageing that emphasise decline (Katz, 1996). Negative stereotypes reinforce the negative understanding of ageing and contribute to the social construction of ageing as a time of dependency and passivity. The individual becomes lost within the drive to classify and segregate on the basis of chronological age.

Make a list of stereotypes of 'old age' and 'ageing'.

What impact do you think these have on:

a) Older people?

b) Social work and health care practitioners?

c) The wider society?

Although there is great diversity within the ageing population, older people have historically been treated as a homogenous group on the basis of their chronological age. Recently there has been a shift in the perception of ageing which demonstrates a recognition of the changing lives of older people (Biggs et al., 2006). This involves an appreciation of the impact of social change and socio-cultural differences on the experiences of ageing in contemporary Britain.

Concern over ageism in UK has 'derived chiefly from worries over the trend in the labour market towards "early exit" of older workers from employment' (Loretto et al., 2000, p. 280). In 2006, The Employment Equality (Age) Regulations came into force protecting workers from age discrimination. It is now illegal for employers to discriminate against employees or job seekers because of their age. However, ageism is far more pervasive than just this 'economic' focus of productivity and employment, and it can affect not only the way older people are seen, but also their access to health and social care provision. Research has shown that older patients receive less medical information from doctors than do their younger patients (Adler et al., 1998). Services for older people tend to be run in poorer environments with less funding than for other groups (Levenson, 2003).

ACTIVITY 4

Think about current health and social care practice. How are older people discriminated against on the basis of their age? What are the implications of this in general in society and specifically in social work practice?

Now think about multiple levels of discrimination, such as ethnicity, gender, sexuality and disability. What impact do multiple levels of discrimination have on older people? If possible draw on your own practice experience to reflect upon this question.

Recent policy in Britain has sought to redefine ageing and blur the boundaries between midlife and old age. Biggs et al. (2006) identify three themes within UK policy discourse which work together to try to redefine the reality of ageing in contemporary society:

1. The shift to wider definitions of 'older people' which encompass the '50 plus' lifecourse has been used increasingly in policy documents such as *Life Begins at 50* (Department of Social Security, 2000) and *Opportunity Age* (Department for Work and Pensions, 2005).

2. The erasure of generational difference (Biggs et al., 2006) and a blurring of the life-course in that there is perceived to be no difference between older people's experiences and needs and those of younger people.

3. A view that 'age is in the mind' (Biggs et al., 2006, p.244). This approach sees age as a problem of attitude.

This approach tends to emphasise the sameness of experience across the lifecourse and, rather than valuing the diversity and special qualities of getting older, it reinforces the fantasies of never growing old. This tendency towards 'agelessness' can be seen as a form of ageism in itself by denying age-based diversity and difference across the lifecourse (Andrews, 1999).

ACTIVITY **5**

Consider the implications for practice of the 'erasure' of generational difference.

What might this mean for service provision, and what might the positive and negative consequences be for service users?

The above discussion illustrates that in contemporary Britain we are at a turning point in the way old age is defined and constructed. While this may go some way to combating age discrimination on the basis of chronological age, we need to be equally aware that a denial of diversity and difference can be oppressive. All older people are subject to the impact of ageism in one form or another, but some are discriminated against further on the basis of their sexuality, gender, ethnicity or disability. In the following chapters you will be encouraged to think critically about current practice with older lesbians and gay men, to consider the implications of heteronormative assumptions, and the impact of fear and isolation on the well-being of older lesbians and gay men.

Chapter 2

Lessons to be drawn from the Gay and Grey research project

By Ann Fannin

Sampling and setting the scene

Many of the volunteers, who had seen the publicity about the proposed research, went along to the initial meetings not really knowing what was in store. Several people thought it was just a case of filling in a couple of questionnaires and that would be that. Some joined through loneliness and isolation, others out of a sense duty to the lesbian and gay community, while others regarded it as an academic challenge with a very fulfilling goal; perhaps for many there was an element of all three reasons.

As time passed it became clear that the volunteers themselves were to be the researchers – albeit with the support of a paid co-ordinator and a university-based researcher. Several volunteers dropped out during the three-year journey for a variety of reasons. Others stayed; for them the experience was incredibly empowering. My own personal journey with my co-researchers in 'Gay and Grey' was enormously rewarding. Some of the one-to-one interviews I did will remain with me for years to come – I was moved to tears with some and joined in laughter with others. I gained new skills and extended existing ones. I learnt what hard work 'consensus' is, and found working with so many people who have different perceptions from mine fascinating (sometimes frustrating – but that was the richness of it all).

One of the great strengths of the project was that it was volunteer-led by older lesbians and gay men themselves. From the outset there was a strong commitment not only among the volunteers but also from the respondents. There was an instinctive feeling from the volunteers that this was an important piece of work and that it could improve the lives of many older lesbians and gay men for future years. Apart from Age Concern's recent publication *Opening Doors* (2001) and a research project into the housing needs of older lesbians and gay men in London undertaken by Polari (River, 2006), little work had been done in this particular field in the UK. A total of 91 people responded to the 300 questionnaires sent out and 30 of those offered to be interviewed individually. Among the volunteer researchers, eight stayed the full three years to complete the work.

At the outset it is important to look closely at the sample on which the research project was based. Despite intensive publicity about the project, 98.9 per cent of respondents were either white British or white other; 44.0 per cent identified themselves as professional, with 22.0 per cent manual/technical and the rest skilled, semi-skilled or unskilled. Not everyone chose to declare their gender but it seems that just over half were women. Two people identified themselves as bisexual and one as transsexual. The samples were found in Bournemouth, Dorset, Hampshire, Devon and Somerset, with 71.4 per cent living in urban areas.

Many older lesbians and gay men are invisible in our society and, as the research confirmed, being homosexual is still fraught with fear, secrecy and apprehension. For some people it is easier to remain firmly 'in the closet'. Older people from races, creeds, cultures, ethnic communities and backgrounds other than the predominant culture can be, and are, particularly vulnerable to homophobia. They suffer dual prejudice, both from homophobia coming from within their own communities and racism from wider society. Racism and prejudice are still, unfortunately, widespread and there is clear evidence of racism within lesbian and gay men's circles. Black issues are frequently ignored within those social and support networks that exist for lesbians and gay men, and it can be a stark choice for individual black gay people to either remain closeted or risk losing their family and friends who exist as a bulwark against a racist society (Hayfield, 1995). To come out as an older lesbian or gay man who is seen to be 'different' in a largely white community, like in the southwest of England (Census, 2001), is problematic and risky for the individual.

The research team recognised quite early on in the project that it would be difficult to find older lesbian and gay people who were willing to risk exposing themselves to scrutiny and they recognised that it was imperative to assure absolute anonymity. They were keen to gather a representative sample of the gay community as a whole and to reach out to those particularly isolated in rural areas and to those who had no experience of being out in the community. For reasons beyond their control they were unable to fulfil their objective completely.

Some people responded to promotional leaflets left in libraries, surgeries and gay venues, others to the advertisements put in local papers. The majority came from 'snowballing' (Morrison, 1988); that is, by word of mouth and with contacts from older lesbian and gay people who were involved with the project from the start. Snowballing is an effective way to reach many people. However, in this instance, it did mean that to some extent the respondents had to be at least tentatively connected with other gay people. We can presume, then, that the sample was made up of people who were more confident in their sexuality than some.

ACTIVITY 1

What issues are involved in sampling minority groups of older people?

Quantitative and qualitative research

The research project was multifaceted, with data being collected both quantitatively and qualitatively (questionnaires and face-to-face interviews.) Semi-structured interviews of approximately one hour allowed an opportunity for the interviewees to talk about broader issues if it was deemed appropriate, while at the same time giving a uniform approach to the interviews. Participatory action research (PAR) (Heron, 1996), which was the form of research chosen for this project, produced a dynamic of its own and a small community development team soon evolved in parallel to those doing the data collection and analysis. In this way practical tasks, such as setting up support groups, compiling a lesbian and gay directory and running IT courses, were able to be done as and when the project became known and needs were identified.

The aim of the questionnaire was to find out some general information about personal situations in the here and now; and to ascertain thoughts, fears, hopes and aspirations for the future as they (the respondents) get older and possibly frailer. It was designed with a series of tick boxes to multiple questions with some open questions for brief comment. The areas looked at were:

- general information
- sexuality
- relationships and social networks
- community and housing
- social care and health
- getting older.

From the results of the questionnaire, the research team was able to tease out the emerging themes and decide on the issues that needed to be looked at in further detail. The areas decided on for the interviews were:

- current lifestyles
- acceptance
- coming out
- needs and aspirations.

Main findings of the research project

Individuality

All older lesbians and gay men are individual and experience their sexuality in different ways.

If the research project did anything, it proved that to be human is a complex business. Each person who responded had experienced life and their sexuality in particular in very different ways. Each person had a distinct history which shaped the way they viewed the world and how they reacted to it. In our society, people tend to be more isolated than years ago. For lesbians and gay men this can be exacerbated by their perceived 'different-ness' and by established homophobia. Many respondents wanted to establish and support existing social groups within the older lesbian and gay community, where they could feel comfortable among other older lesbian and gay people.

In recent years, views on homosexuality have relaxed. In Britain and many other Western countries, it is no longer illegal to be a homosexual. With the passing of the Civil Partnership Act (2004), a same-sex couple can register as a civil partnership and have equal treatment in a wide range of legal matters to married couples. The Equality Act (2006) makes discrimination against lesbians and gay men in the provision of goods and services illegal.

The three-year Gay and Grey project highlighted many things. Some of the respondents felt positive about being who they were. 'Coming out' for some had been a liberating and empowering experience. When they took the courage to come out, many were surprised that people were much more accepting than they had feared. Others felt negative about the future and many had encountered devastating acts of homophobia.

Many older lesbians and gay men, however, grew up in an era when fear of being 'found out' was a constant anxiety and the cult of secrecy was the norm. In an atmosphere where homophobia is embedded institutionally, it is almost impossible not to assimilate these views internally; this is known as 'internalised homophobia' (Rivers, 2004). Many people in our survey had experienced a lot of hostility and verbal and physical abuse in their lives while many had not. However, as we shall see in the next section, nearly all felt ill at ease about coming out to all people. To be homosexual in the twenty-first century is still not easy.

ACTIVITY 2

Do you feel that passing laws to make homophobic discrimination illegal will eradicate prejudice against lesbians and gay men?

Continuing process

Coming out is a continuing process throughout lesbians' and gay men's lives. Some find it easier than others. Very few people feel at ease coming out to all people. Sometimes it is more difficult for older people. Fear of isolation and/or hostility from others is a contributing factor.

Probably one of the most important issues examined in the research was that of sexuality. The question-naire strove to study personal experiences of being a lesbian or a gay man. Some of the results were revealing. Several respondents (16.4 per cent) had

I realised my sexuality before I married – it was a bit of a nightmare and my parents threatened to make me a ward of court and you know – it was just hell. (Lifting the Lid, 2006, p.45)

been married and raised a family; many had come out in later life. Socialisation of hetero-sexism in our society is remarkably strong. Even today there is an all-embracing expectancy that sons and daughters will grow up, have relationships with the opposite sex and repro-duce their own 'nuclear family'. In the 1940s, 1950s and 1960s, while in their formative years, any deviation by individuals from this ideal was viewed with suspicion and anxiety. Some of the interviewees told of parental angst if they even suspected their sons or daughters of being gay. Some were sent for psychiatric 'help', others were thrown out of home or systematically browbeaten into conformity. Many people spoke of their teenage years when they had no understanding of what it meant to be gay or lesbian; it was never talked about in public. Some spoke of feeling 'different' but not being able to know why. It became clear from the respondents' stories that most had repressed and secret sexual lives, and many were unable to identify themselves as homosexual until well into maturity.

*I just thank God I'm gay and my mother does – it's never ever been an issue with my family, my grandparents, aunts and uncles, not an issue at all. (*Lifting the Lid, *2006, p.46)*

However, when asked about the impact of their sex-uality on life in general, 48.4 per cent of the respondents said that being a lesbian or a gay man had been a positive experience, 23.1 per cent said it had been negative and 17.8 per cent said it had had no impact; 11.0 per cent did not answer. One person said that to be gay was 'very liberating', another that she felt more fulfilled and happier when living her life as a lesbian and another felt that being gay made him a stronger and more independent person.

On the other hand, there were others who felt like outsiders and had fears of not belong-ing to conventional society. It was obvious that past experiences had a major influence on how they felt about being lesbian or gay. Evidently, parental acceptance in their early years had an effect on their confidence to be 'out' in public. More research into reasons why some people feel more at ease with their sexuality than others would be beneficial. The complexities of what makes us who we are can be daunting and further inquiry would need to embrace the personal, political and social structures in our society; exploration around the effects of homophobia need closer examination if we are to move forward to a more equitable society.

Coming out is a continuous process of negotiation and deciding on a daily basis as to whether it is worth the risk of revealing myself. (Gay and Grey research respondent)

To many heterosexual people, talking about family life, boyfriends, wives, husbands and sex, or to talk about their social lives, is natural. It is assumed that everyone is heterosexual; it is assumed to be the 'natural' state. For lesbians and gay men, talking about home and social life means that they invariably have to come out in almost every conversation. Many homosexual people are anxious about revealing their sexuality and some will go as far as weaving elaborate stories to get round the necessity of declaring their sexuality.

During the interviews and the completion of the questionnaires there was a variety of responses. However, generally there is a picture of discomfort, fear or anxiety about coming out.

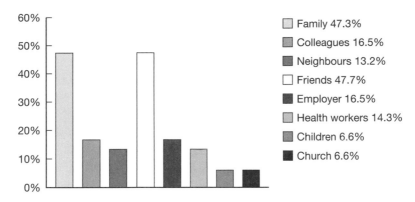

Figure 4 *Who knows your sexuality?*

Figure 4 is an amalgamation of eight separate graphs in the Gay and Grey report dealing with the questions about whom the respondents had told of their sexuality. It shows only those who had told all in these particular categories; 48.4 per cent of the sample had no children. However, the percentage of people who had told their children was remarkably small. There was a similar response to the question about coming out to religious communities. Many did not go to church but, among those who did, very few had come out to their church communities.

These results place the problem of coming out into stark focus and we have to presume significant implications for individuals' emotional and mental well-being. For homosexual people there is a continuing dilemma and it gets no easier as they reach old age. The 'coming out' debate surfaced many times in the interviews. Several people commented that in old age it would probably be easier just to 'go back into the closet' than have to grapple with the issue on a daily basis.

Gay-specific services

A significant percentage of older lesbians and gay men would like to have dedicated lesbian and gay services should they need help and support; most want their sexuality to be taken into account.

'I hope (in old age) that none of my identity, none of who I am is amputated and that includes my sexuality and my sexual needs – from playful flirting, to making love with women.' (Lifting the Lid, 2006, p.37)

In the twenty-first century, the majority of older people manage to get through old age as independent and healthy people well into their 80s and more (Harris, 1997). Many continue to have a healthy sex life and enjoy life to the full; 75.4 per cent of the respondents to the Gay and Grey questionnaire said they still had sexual needs (*Lifting the Lid*, 2006). Established ageism that exists in our society marginalises the old, and part of this marginalisation is the belief that older people are asexual (McGlone and Fitzgerald, 2004). Part of being human is to be sexual. If the assumption is that older people are asexual, they are lumped together as a homogenous group rather than vibrant individuals with sexual desires and social needs. As people get older it is important to respect them as individuals and make sure that their needs are catered for as much as possible. For gay people there is an additional dimension: the assumption of heterosexualism, which makes it even more difficult to hold onto their sexual identity as they get older.

Home care, residential and sheltered housing

The social care and health section of the questionnaire dealt with care preferences. People were asked to state the kind of care and/or services they would prefer if they needed support. Further on in the book there is a section that goes into more detail about different care settings and preferences. The type of care and support given, either at home or in residential homes, is crucial to retaining human dignity and independence. For minority groups, these needs require a little more scrutiny and, for lesbians and gay men in particular, these can be hidden. It is therefore important not to make generalised assumptions.

Although exclusive gay care sounds appealing it is not a good thing in that it isolates older gay people from the community rather than integrating them into society where homophobia will not be tolerated. (Lifting the Lid, 2006. p. 26)

In total, 26.5 per cent said they would prefer gay-designated care homes. Almost 80 per cent wanted 'gay-friendly' homes; that is, they wanted their sexuality to be taken into account and for it to be recognised and validated. They also wanted to be accepted and treated as normal by all staff with whom they came in contact. The anxiety of having to go into a home *per se* was exacerbated by the fear of homophobic prejudice and the assumption of heterosexuality.

As one lesbian pointed out in one of the interviews, much of the banter that goes on between carers and nurses invariably involves heterosexual repartee and innuendo:

As a lesbian I would find this very difficult to deal with – I realise that humour plays an important part in communication, especially in potentially embarrassing situations such as personal care, but it would need to be appropriate to my sexuality otherwise it would make it all so much worse. (Gay and Grey interview participant, 2005)

Home care

Similar kinds of anxieties came up when speaking about home care, with 36.3 per cent preferring a dedicated service of lesbian and gay carers. The majority wanted assurance that any carers who came into the privacy of their homes would know about their sexuality and be at ease with their lifestyle and culture. Home is where we relax and can be ourselves. We have books, pictures, photos and artefacts around that reflect who we are. Older lesbians and gay men need to know that carers would be free of prejudice and comfortable in the surroundings.

It is very important to have cultural visibility – photos, books and art – which are crucial to my identity and therefore my self-esteem.

My main concern would be that my carer would understand and respect my sexuality. (Lifting the Lid, 2006. p. 29)

Sheltered housing

There appeared to be more concerns about possible discrimination and prejudice within sheltered housing, with 40.7 per cent wanting dedicated sheltered housing blocks. Over 80 per cent wanted their sexuality to be taken into account. Many were anxious about homophobia from other residents and were nervous of feeling trapped in close proximity. Others felt that it would be good to have a sheltered housing unit set up specifically for lesbians and gay men.

It would be nice to be in a mixed gay community after living among heterosexuals all my life.

I do worry about homophobia in the wider world. (Lifting the Lid, 2006. p. 30)

ACTIVITY 3

In what ways do older lesbians and gay men suffer from 'multiple discrimination'?

Health and public services

On a scale of 1–5, 52 per cent of people who filled in the questionnaires felt it was very important to have lesbian- and gay-specific health information while only 6.6 per cent felt it wasn't important at all. When asked whether gay-specific information was available, 52.7 per cent said they didn't know and only 24.2 per cent said yes. Considerably more men than women were aware: 42.1 per cent of the men and only 8.7 per cent of the women.

It is worth looking a little deeper into the health issues for older lesbians and gay men. Is there indeed a need for specific information? What are the health issues?

- Lesbians, gay men and bisexuals have a higher instance of mental health problems than the wider population (King and McKeown, 2003).

- It is generally accepted that the reason for this is the discrimination, prejudice and oppression experienced by lesbians, gay men or bisexual people and the level of stigma attached to being gay (Herek, 1991). The effect can erode self-esteem, result in internalised homophobia and lead to a suppression of sexual expression. In addition, McFarlane (1998) highlights a level of homophobia and prejudice within the mental health services themselves that compounds any problems gay people may have. Most lesbians, gay men and bisexuals who were interviewed for this study said they would prefer gay-specific mental health counselling, help and support.

- The use and misuse of tobacco and alcohol are significantly higher among gay people (Age Concern, 2007). As with mental health issues, the problems of alcohol and smoking could be linked to the stress of having to deal with prejudice and homophobia; or that much of lesbians' and gay men's social life, until recently, has been limited to public houses and a drinking culture.

- According to Age Concern (2007), more that 10 per cent of HIV positive men are over 50. The issue of HIV/AIDS is emotive and must be treated with caution. Many gay men have suffered harassment and discrimination encouraged by the myth that most gay men are HIV positive – while in reality HIV predominantly affects heterosexual people (King and McKeown, 2003). However, in the Gay and Grey research interviews, there were several gay men who were either HIV positive or who had been deeply affected by HIV/AIDS, with many having had partners, boyfriends and close friends die of the disease. HIV/AIDS had devastating consequences within the gay community in the early 1980s when it first developed, as gay men were the first to be affected in the West. Because of the general stigma attached to HIV/AIDS (National Aids Trust, 2007) and the discrimination towards gay men, it is vital to have specialist health professionals and counsellors available, particularly for older gay men who suffered much in the earlier years before effective medication was developed.

Older lesbians are generally invisible in our society and have been marginalised and unacknowledged where medical and sexual matters are concerned. It has been assumed, both by medical practitioners and by many lesbians themselves, that because they have sex only with other women they are immune from contracting sexual diseases. Women can and do exchange body fluids and it is important that they have access to safe sex information (Fish, 2005). Internal examinations and cancer smears can be very uncomfortable for those who are technically virgin. Many lesbians wrongly believe that they are also immune to cervical cancer and can neglect to have regular checks. Again, doctors and nurses frequently assume heterosexual activity and can make inappropriate comments that are embarrassing. Many lesbians, it seems, have experienced male violence in the past and thus feel uneasy in the presence of male practitioners. These issues are rarely taken into account in the health service, which means that lesbians are less likely than their heterosexual counterparts to seek medical advice. According to Stonewall (2007a, b) and Carr et al. (1999), the health needs of lesbians are a particularly neglected area of health care research.

Bereavement counselling

Inevitably through life we all experience the loss of a loved one and, as people get older, the experiences are more frequent. The issue of bereavement came up a lot in the interviews for the Gay and Grey project. The loss of a loved one or partner is desperately hard to come to terms with, but for lesbians and gay men it is doubly difficult because there is a constant battle for recognition that gay relationships are equally as close, loving and important as those of heterosexual partnerships. Added to this, there is the constant need to come out and explain the situation during the process of bereavement. Unthinking discrimination and assumptions can make things very painful.

Below we have taken extracts from two interviews to illustrate the point. Both discuss aspects of bereavement and grief. The first is from a gay man:

> *I used to be quite socially active I suppose. I belonged to a couple of motorcycle clubs and so on, but it was all very shallow especially after my last partner died eight years ago, and I got absolutely no response whatsoever, not one person from these clubs showed any sympathy...so since my partner died I haven't really gone out very much at all; in fact, after he died, I hardly went outside the door for a year, I went into a sort of deep, deep depression...I had bereavement counselling through my GP. It was helpful I suppose; it got me through...that was the hardest thing I think it was that people*

didn't realise...that bereavement in a gay relationship could be so brutal, you know, and hard...so that was probably the worst time I can remember. (Lifting the Lid, 2006, pp.64–5)

Further on in the interview this man said that, in retrospect, it might have been much easier if the counselling had been gay-specific.

In the next extract, a woman speaks of the need for specific counselling for lesbian and gay people. After her partner died, she was offered bereavement counselling and she describes the first group session she had with other (heterosexual) people:

...and what they do is they subdivide you into smaller groups of four or five...and you just get an opportunity to tell your story. And I mean there is no guarantee that people are going to be accepting...they are caught up with their own stuff and probably not listening terribly well, I certainly wasn't listening to them...but it's hard, and what it does is it puts something else on the table, which actually isn't my agenda at the time...it puts homosexuality on the table, when actually all that I care about is the fact that my partner's died and I am hurting. So that was a bit uncomfortable and I just – I would have preferred to have been with other gay people. I didn't mind that it was mixed gender, but I would have preferred to have been with other gay people...Somehow I would have liked there to have been some kind of acknowledgment of my relationship with my partner...I think more than anything else there is a need for gay bereavement counselling... (Lifting the Lid, 2006, p.65)

ACTIVITY 4

How do you think medical and mental health provision could ensure that the specific needs of older lesbians, gay men and bisexuals are addressed?

The need for social outlets

Lesbians and gay men want their sexuality to be validated in a society that is deemed heterosexual; they need and want a 'gay-friendly' society and to be accepted as a normal part of the community. However, many also want/need social outlets to enable them to meet with other lesbians and gay men for recreation and leisure.

During the course of the three-year Gay and Grey research project, respondents, volunteers and interviewees talked of an 'ideal world': a world where they could go about their lives without having to look over their shoulders or be wary of what they say; a world where they are accepted for who they

We just wanted to be treated the same as everyone else. (Lifting the Lid, 2006, p.66)

are and not for whom they love; a world where their sexuality is as normal and as valid as anyone else's. This world, all agreed, is a long way off. And as we have seen, homophobia and prejudice are unfortunately still widespread. Until such a time as the 'ideal world' is attained, many gay people need havens in which to be themselves.

One of the needs identified during the research project was for social outlets for older lesbians and gay men. In Dorset, where this project was carried out, older lesbians have, over the years, developed a well-established and vibrant group with over a 100 members. They have a variety of activities which means that there is plenty going on locally for those women who are socially confident and physically able. Gay men have not been so lucky. Quite soon into the project it was realised that there was little for older gay men except pubs and clubs where many no longer wanted to be. Gay and Grey volunteers supported older local gay men to get groups started but this proved difficult. It appears that men do not easily organise themselves and there is much work to be done if a men's group is to be successful.

Many of the interviewees pointed to the lack of places for older gay people to go and were eager to come up with suggestions. Some suggested gay drop-in centres or quiet wine or coffee bars where they could pop in for a chat. Others wanted specific clubs like gardening groups or fishing outings, walking groups and art appreciation. Only 15.4 per cent regarded themselves as having a very active social life and 74 per cent said that they would like to have more opportu-

...it'd be nice to have a club, which had a quiet section or a lounge with chairs. (Lifting the Lid, 2006, p.42)

nities to meet others. For some older people on low incomes or with poor mobility, it is hard to get out. Lack of reliable public transport was cited as an added difficulty, especially in rural areas. Some suggested advocacy groups or buddying schemes for those who are housebound. On a scale of 1 to 5, when asked how isolated they felt, 8.8 per cent said they felt totally isolated and only 39.6 per cent felt not at all. Significantly more men than women felt totally isolated, and fewer men were 'not at all' isolated.

ACTIVITY 5

Why do you think it is important for older lesbians and gay men to have their own social support networks?

Education and training

Education and training are of paramount importance; meaningful equality statements should not only be enshrined in all statutory and independent bodies' policies, but must be followed up with meaningful ways to ensure that they are adhered to. Older lesbian and gay issues should be given a higher public profile to enable others to obtain information on gay issues.

In parallel with the survey, the group established links with many service providers: the police, local health authorities, council and housing workers, the Citizens Advice Bureau, the Samaritans, Age Concern and lot of other interested bodies. Networking was regarded as important for Gay and Grey and they met with a variety of different groups to share information and to publicise the project. It was clear that many people in all areas, be it charitable, voluntary, statutory or independent, were keen to learn about the project. For many, it was the first time they'd thought about the issue.

By producing its paper *Equality and Diversity: The Way Ahead* (2006), the government has stated a commitment towards equality and the consultation process is in progress. To make it happen in a meaningful way much has to be done, not only through legislation but also in terms of training and education. Other minority and disadvantaged groups – gender, age, race and disability – have been recognised as important for many years; sexual orientation has been a recent addition and the issues not clearly defined. Ageism is institutionally embedded in our society (Age Concern, 2007) and, within this, older gay people's identities and needs are lost.

Education, education, education

Make sure they have a ploicy in place which aims to discover client sexuality and to ensure they are treated equally and respected equally. (Lifting the Lid, 2006, p.31)

Nearly all the respondents to the survey felt that it was essential that all staff should have awareness training. To ensure that services are inclusive and that gay people are integrated into society without prejudice, much work has to be done throughout the service industries.

Several people wanted older lesbian and gay issues opened up into the public domain. This would not only give gay people a higher profile, but would give greater confidence to those who were isolated. There were many ideas, like putting pamphlets in libraries, articles in the media, posters and literature in highly visible places, more positive images of older gay people in advertisements, art and television. In other words, many older gay people want to become a visible and positive part of society without prejudice and the assumption of heterosexuality.

ACTIVITY 6

Given the current sensitivity around the issue of homosexuality, how would you go about designing a policy that aims to discover a client's sexuality?

Conclusion

It is estimated that around 7 per cent of the population is gay (Stonewall, 2007a, b). Given that many lesbians, gay men and bisexuals are invisible in our society, there is no accurate way of knowing if this is correct. Indeed, it is questionable whether sexuality can ever be sorted neatly into boxes. Some feel their sexuality to be genetically determined (Turner, 1995); others see sexuality as a fluid and changeable emotion. As far back as the 1940s, Alfred Kinsey, the controversial sexologist, put forward the notion of an eight-point scale, where 0 was considered predominantly heterosexual and 7 predominantly homosexual, with varying degrees between (he had an additional scale X for those who didn't have any sexual desire) (Kinsey et al., 1948 and Kinsey,1953). What is indisputable is that lesbians, gay men and bisexuals make up a significant part of the world population. The issue then is very important.

Despite the difficulties of getting a truly representative sample of respondents and interviewees for the research, Gay and Grey successfully gathered a relatively comprehensive and useful picture of what it means to be an older lesbian, gay man or a bisexual person in the twenty-first century. Being homosexual is still fraught with internal personal emotions and external prejudice from society, and in some ways this is a circular problem. As we have seen, many lesbians, gay men and bisexuals are fearful of a hostile world and therefore remain silent about their sexuality. By remaining invisible in mainstream society, the issues remain marginalised. Prejudice and bigotry thrive in an atmosphere of fear and ignorance and in a divided society. For many years, the state reinforced a division by criminalising or demonising homosexuals. For decades, lesbians, gay men and bisexuals have campaigned tirelessly, demanding equality. Recent changes in legislation provide a framework for things to improve.

The Gay and Grey project showed that all gay people experience their sexuality in different ways and have different needs and aspirations; it proved that being human is a complex business. Just as the assumption of heterosexuality can lead to discrimination and oppression, assumptions that all gay people have the same needs could lead to misunderstandings.

For many older gay people, the effects of growing up in a society where it was illegal to be homosexual has been traumatic and destructive. Because most suffer from a degree of internalised homophobia and have maybe suffered overt discrimination, they feel anxious about their advancing years and worry about calling on care services which may be unsympathetic or unaware of their needs.

As one woman summarised, '*In addition to the concerns of all people as they get older – declining health, strength, independence – there is an increased risk of social and emotional isolation by belonging to a minority group in society*' (Lifting the Lid, 2006, front cover).

All those who were involved in the Gay and Grey project as volunteers – in data collection, developing groups, networking with agencies, organising IT courses or participating in the interviews and questionnaires – were over 50 years old. Most were in their 60s or 70s, one or two in their 90s. Choosing participatory action research as the method of inquiry proved empowering both for the researchers and the participants; it embraced a lot of people and, to a greater or lesser extent, increased their confidence personally. Ultimately, their work has gone some way to improving gay people's lives for the future. However, there is still much to be done to eradicate homophobia in the here-and-now.

Priorities for the future

- A commitment to help provide gay-friendly services and to develop social outlets
- To encourage the setting up of meaningful equality statements
- To support ongoing training/awareness courses for all staff
- Not to assume everyone is heterosexual
- To place gay-specific information in public places
- To create the use of the internet for communication and research
- To commission and/or support continued research into lesbian, gay and bisexual issues.

ACTIVITY 7

What one thing do you think you could do to help eradicate homophobia in our society?

Chapter 3

Aspects of homophobia and heterosexuality in later life: personal, cultural, structural

By Christina Hicks

Heterosexuality is not normal, it's just common. (Dorothy Parker, 1893–1967)

The results of the Gay and Grey in Dorset (2006) study, *Lifting the Lid on Sexuality and Ageing*, add to the small but increasing body of evidence which shows that older lesbians and gay men are a diverse and varied group who experience their sexuality in many different ways and that their aspirations are not dissimilar to those of any older person. Any fears they may have about increasing frailty and needing health and/or social care have the added dimension of their sexuality and how that might be viewed. Included in the key themes identified by the research are that personal identity is important and that isolation and exclusion are common experiences. Also identified is an overwhelming need for acceptance, understanding and equality as well as a continuing fear of homophobia and isolation in an alien world.

In her paper 'Developing anti-oppressive empowering social work practice with older lesbian women and gay men', Jackie Langley (2001) reports how older lesbians and gay men perceive their needs as they age and possibly become ill. She highlights the unifying theme of oppression and the expressed need of lesbians and gay men for acceptance. Their identification of discrimination as an important issue is also highlighted. This study used a similar methodology to that of the Gay and Grey project, the main difference between the two being the inclusion in Langley's study of the issue and impact of HIV/AIDS.

The study carried out three years later by Heaphy et al. (2004) looks at how being non-heterosexual affects the ways in which people experience ageing and later life. It also pays attention to the ways in which non-heterosexuals negotiate personal ageing. It highlights the difficulties of being able to find non-heterosexual groups when getting older and the additional problems faced by those who live outside urban areas. Of interest was the finding that women considered the lesbian 'community' to be less ageist than heterosexuals and gay males; gay men believed that their community placed a great emphasis on youth and appearance. The point is also made that there is no one experience or model for understanding lesbian and gay male ageing.

In their paper 'Policy implications of ageing sexualities', Heaphy and Yip (2006) develop further their previous research outlined above and state that the 'heteronormative values' which underpin policy and law 'lead to a sense of social exclusion among older lesbians and gay men'. They go on to argue that, despite recent legislation, older lesbians and gay men still consider themselves to 'have diminished recognition and rights in policy and law' (p.450).

The findings of the Gay and Grey research, in the main, accord with and further develop those of these previous studies. The difficulty of identifying a representative sample of a hidden population of older lesbians and gay men is identified by all the researchers, who also emphasise the relevance of the information gathered and the diversity of experience.

That the aspirations of older lesbians and gay men are rarely achieved is due not only to the continuing existence of homophobia but also, and in no small part, to a general and deeply embedded assumption of heterosexuality. The National Service Framework for Older People (Department of Health, 2004) specifically identifies minority groups regarded as older, but fails to include older lesbians and gay men. This underlines their invisibility in policies and subsequently increases their invisibility in practice. This is highlighted by Heaphy et al. (2004, p.882), who state that older lesbians and gay men remain, '"invisible" in political, policy and advocacy discourses on ageing and old age'. How often do you see positive and affirming references to the value and significance of the lives of older lesbians and gay men? At most there may be a grudging lip service to their existence. This is also identified by Langley (2001), who states that oppression and invisibility are central to the lives of lesbians and gay men. In addition, there is the homogeneity and invisibility that all older people experience due to ageism. So, older lesbians and gay men not only face direct discrimination through a combination of homophobia and ageism but also, and more commonly, through the 'subtle indirect pervasiveness of heterosexism' (Logan and Kershaw, 1994, p.62). Heterosexism is defined as believing that one kind of loving is superior and therefore has a right to be dominant.

In their paper 'Empowering older people, beyond the care model' (2001), Thompson and Thompson point out that, as social work derives its roots from a medical model, it is generally assumed that older people need to be cared for or looked after in some way. This presupposes that old age equates to illness and disability whereas, in the main, older people are no less healthy and active, both physically and mentally, then many younger people. It also precludes the recognition of the broader needs and rights of the individual. They propose a framework for the development of forms of practice with older people that could empower individuals and place social workers as facilitators or enablers. Three levels that could be explored are put forward for consideration.

1. **Personal**. This relates to the personal level of power; that is, the individual's ability to influence other people and the circumstances he or she faces. It includes confidence, communication and other interpersonal skills. It recognises personal empowerment as a prerequisite for other forms of empowerment. It also applies collectively as well as individually, in that it does not have to be limited to an individual; it can be a shared experience.

2. **Cultural**. This refers to the level of shared meanings and therefore to power in terms of discourses, which carry with them sets of assumptions, stereotypes, language, imagery and so on. The subtle and commonly negative portrayal of older people becomes so accepted that it seems invisible and loses its impact, thus helping to perpetuate established patterns of power and inequality.

3. **Structural**. Power derives not only from personal skills and influences or established discourses, but also patterns of inequality and the social locations associated with them. Age, like class, race and gender, operates as a form of social division – it categorises people and assigns them to a particular social position. This plays a significant role in maintaining the social order.

Just as a lack of awareness and understanding of ageism can be a barrier to enabling empowerment of older people generally, an additional and similar lack of knowledge of the effects of heterosexism can mitigate against successful working with older lesbians and gay men. If the model expressed by Thompson and Thompson is applied to working with older lesbians and gay men, it can support the exploration of ways of being truly inclusive and non-discriminatory.

ACTIVITY 1

On your own, or with a friend or colleague, think about the older people in your life – relatives, friends or neighbours – and write down any ways in which, because of their age, you have:

- *been embarrassed by their behaviour or thought it inappropriate*

- *assumed you know what they need*

- *taken over and made decisions for them.*

Now think about why you behaved or thought in those ways and what impact there may have been. What does it tell you about yourself and your attitudes?

If there are ways in which you consider work practices display ageist and/or heterosexist views, what are they and how might you change them?

Personal

The Gay and Grey study and others have demonstrated that each person experiences their sexuality differently. At best, it can be positive and life-enhancing; at worst it can result in 'devastating exposure to cruel and thoughtless discrimination' (Gay and Grey in Dorset, 2006, p.20). For most, it is likely to be somewhere between these two extremes, although at any time they may experience great joy and fulfilment or direct discrimination and harassment.

In the same way as a constant barrage of negative stereotypes of age can lead to a subjective, internalised oppression (Thompson and Thompson, 2001), so many older lesbians and gay men have developed an internalised homophobia that influences their responses and ability to be open about themselves. It is possible for someone to perceive an adverse reaction in another person when it does not exist; in fact there may be total acceptance or even no comprehension of their sexuality. Nevertheless, the perception is real and can have a negative and debilitating effect upon social interaction and the ability to develop friendships.

While age in itself does not necessarily bring poor health, older people are, nevertheless, more likely to develop an increasing need for both health and social care. As Hinchliff et al. (2004) have shown in their article 'I daresay I might find it embarrassing', there has been little study of general practitioner (GP) attitudes to lesbians and gay men. As they point out, it was only in 1973 that homosexuality was declassified as a psychiatric disorder and it seems that there is a continuing link between homosexuality and abnormality in the medical profession. They cite a number of studies that show the fear of disclosure and the negative effect this can have on treatment.

The question asked by the Department of Health 'What do you want from the NHS?' received the response '*What I want is for the NHS to realise that some older people are gay or lesbian...and to make services sensitive to us and appropriate to us.*' It also produced some responses that are equally applicable to lesbians and gay men of all ages, for example: '*When I go to the doctor I want it not to matter that I'm not heterosexual*' and '*I'm sick of GPs and other medical staff asking inappropriate questions about my personal life*' (Department of Health, 2006b).

In itself, the need to consult with a medical practitioner can create a level of stress that could be considerably exacerbated by an underlying concern about the probable need to 'come out'. This can lead to a reluctance to consult a GP, thus delaying diagnosis and treatment. If the condition is such that input from other members of the care team is likely to be necessary, there may be a fear that if they do 'come out', the knowledge of their sexuality might become known in the local community. The lack of knowledge of lesbian and gay male lifestyles is apparent in a great many doctors and health care workers generally, as identified by Hinchliff et al. (2004), which adds to the problems of consulting openly about health and care matters. So, older lesbians and gay men may have experienced or witnessed negative, or even hostile, attitudes in their encounters with health and social care professionals. When consultations and meetings are conducted on the assumption that there is or has been an opposite-sex spouse or partner, it creates an issue that either has to be confronted or 'gone along with'. However, if the assumption of heterosexuality is removed, the climate is potentially much more open to an individual feeling comfortable about volunteering information about their sexuality.

Trotter and Hafford-Letchfield (2006) stated that, although it was once considered to be a private and personal issue, sexuality is now 'accepted as a public, political and even fashionable issue' and that 'sexuality is linked to what we do and to the status attributed within publicly visible social structures...'. They also state that in social work it is essential that there is a chance to discuss sexuality. Almost a decade earlier, Berkman and Zinberg (1997) were identifying the fact that there is evidence that social workers may be biased when dealing with lesbians and gay men, that despite their training, they are susceptible to 'absorbing the explicit and implicit biases held by mainstream society' (p.319). They note that homophobic attitudes in social workers and counsellors make them 'less effective, if not actually harmful, in delivering social services to gay and lesbian clients' (p.320). They also highlight the fact that people who are not considered to be homophobic can be heterosexist, which can adversely influence their attitudes towards lesbians and gay men: 'Gay male and lesbian populations have historically been seen not simply as different from but as somehow less than their heterosexual counterparts' (p.319). They concluded that research was needed to enable better understanding about the role of social work education in reducing homophobia and hetereosexism. The need for awareness training to be developed was clearly identified in the Gay and Grey research results.

There is also the danger of falling into the trap of what Langley (2001) describes as a '"sexually blind" approach' (p.920). She suggests that homophobia and heterosexism are 'points on a continuum' and that further along that continuum is what she calls 'liberal humanism' (p.920). This outwardly expresses tolerance or acceptance but acts oppressively in denying the differences of lesbian and gay experience, which results in unfair actions.

The Gay and Grey research (2006) showed that while the aspirations of older and lesbians and gay men are much the same as those of everyone else, their differing experiences militate against them achieving those aspirations, in addition to the way ageism does against all older people.

Added to the disempowerment of age, homophobia and heterosexism can be the experience of a work history that has been marred by an inability to be open about one's sexuality or by the rejection that can follow such openness. So, there are many older lesbians and gay men who find themselves financially less secure having been unable to obtain, or maintain, occupations that give a good salary and pension. Also, many older lesbians and gay men have had heterosexual relationships because this was the only socially acceptable arrangement available to them; it also enabled them to hide their sexuality. The part marriage has played is also highlighted by Langley (2001), where she explores the meaning of 'family' and how many older lesbians and gay men have spent their lives 'passing' (as heterosexual) or being 'closeted'.

For older lesbians who married and had children, an absence from the workplace while caring for the family thus reduced further their earning power and pension development. Lack of income as well as being property-rich and cash-poor can affect everyone. It can lead some women in particular to enter into relationships that are based primarily on 'resources' because, with the added dimension of the historical imbalance in earnings between men and women, when alone they find themselves living in real poverty and isolation. Such relationships can, in themselves, however, be stressful and lead to other problems. Just as in a heterosexual relationship, if they fail and there is a jointly-owned property, the proceeds of which have to be shared, the outcome can be homelessness and greater poverty and seclusion. For the older lesbian or gay man there is also the prospect of social exclusion because of their sexuality (Heaphy and Yip, 2006).

27

We live in a society where status is related to occupation and income, with retirement generally being seen as having low status and people who are dependent on state benefits having even less status. There can be a reluctance to claim benefits, particularly those that are means tested, not only because of a perceived stigma but also because a greater disclosure about personal circumstances is required. Inadequate income and increasing frailty also impact upon mobility and access to transport, which in turn impacts upon the ability to socialise. Low income, low status, poor or no transport can all result in low self-esteem and/or poor physical and mental health. All these plus fear of discrimination because of sexuality can add to the problems faced in later life. Any or all have the potential to limit access to services and social activities, significantly affecting the ability of the individual to influence their circumstances.

ACTIVITY 2

Think about and write down the possible negative effects of retirement on lifestyle and self-esteem.

Other than retirement, in what ways is legal/institutional ageism manifested?

Think about how you would like to live in your old age, then imagine being old and frail, and write down what impact you think that would have on your chosen lifestyle; what differences would being lesbian or gay make?

Do you consider that you are influenced by knowledge of someone's work history or income and, if you are, in what ways does this affect your attitude to them and to your work practices?

Cultural

The introduction of the Sexual Offences Act in 1967, which legalised sex in private between two consenting adults over the age of 21, moved towards a level of equality for gay men which was further progressed by the vote in 1994 by the House of Commons to reduce the age of consent to 18. It is true that in the UK the climate for lesbians and gay men has changed over the last decade and the introduction of the Civil Partnership Act 2004 gives lesbian and gay couples the same rights and responsibilities as married heterosexual couples, including joint treatment for income-related benefits and joint state pension benefits. Also, the Equality Act (Sexual Orientation) Regulations 2007 makes it unlawful for anyone in any profession on all levels, including the voluntary sector, to discriminate in the provision of goods and services on the grounds of sexual orientation. Nevertheless, it must be remembered that people over 55 have lived in a climate of homophobia and discrimination all their lives and, as Heaphy and Yip (2006) point out, it takes a long time for legal reform to 'filter down to more specialised areas of policy and practice' (p.449); it can take even longer to change social attitudes.

Something as ordinary as moving home can be fraught with fears for lesbians and gay men about how new neighbours will respond if their sexuality becomes known. When changing GP practice, the decision has to be made about whether to declare their sexuality. It is the same if faced with changing health/social care teams whether through moving location or varying needs. Even joining a local choir, enrolling at a gym or becoming involved with the local walking, drama or social group requires a choice to be made about whether or not to 'come out'. One woman interviewed for the Gay and Grey research stated: '*As an older lesbian I am more invisible, less of a threat, therefore more easily accepted in my local community*' (Gay and Grey in Dorset, 2006, p.35). But this implies that it is necessary to dissemble and possibly live in fear of discovery and what may happen as a result.

At the time their paper was published, Logan and Kershaw (1994) noted that, while race and gender were prominent features of social work course curricula, mere lip service was being paid to sexual orientation – any such interest was primarily associated with HIV/AIDS. Although an important issue in itself, such focus serves only to perpetuate the perceived 'otherness' of homosexuality.

It was highlighted by Heaphy et al. (2004) that it is increasingly being recognised that social and cultural differences are important in how diversity of ageing experiences are shaped. Also highlighted is the lack of studies of older lesbians and gay men and their experiences of ageing. Their article concludes that there are several reasons why older non-heterosexuals should be given more attention. They include the increasing public acceptance of homosexuality that has led more people to lead openly non-heterosexual lives. Also, the lesbian and gay male populations have developed distinctive ways of living so are likely to face unprecedented challenges as they age. The issue is likely to become more visible as the generation of lesbian and gay activists from the 1960s and 1970s enter old age.

Negative experiences of declaring one's sexuality can, and often do, create an internalised homophobia. This in turn can 'lead to isolation, which over time leads to exclusion from communities, opportunities and services' (Gay and Grey in Dorset, 2006, p.19). With older gay men in particular there is a lived history of homosexual illegality which leads many to live in fear, hiding their true sexuality. Many older lesbians have also experienced discrimination, persecution, removal of their children and exclusion from the family and religious community: '*...some members of my family...regard my sexuality as an illness, or due to childhood damage*' (p.19).

Gateway to Heaven, Clare Summerskill's play about the experiences of older lesbians and gay men (a film version is available on DVD from Age Concern, 2007), is a powerful portrayal of life from the 1940s and 1950s through to the 1970s which illustrates graphically the lived experiences of many older lesbians and gay men. It is important that such experiences and their impact are recognised and taken into account, not only by health and social care professionals but by everyone who may be in a position to influence services.

A fear that is probably common to everyone as they age is the possibility of needing personal and/or residential care. Given the assumption of heterosexuality and the existence of ageism and homophobia, the prospect of being placed in a situation where all talk and references are to marriage and children, and where there is no shared experience that can be called upon in daily conversation, can cause the gay person to shun help. This is true of both care in the home and care in residential establishments. Most conversations with older people seem to assume there is, or was, a spouse and enquire about occupation, background, offspring and siblings. This can cause real pain to some individuals who have had a bad reaction to declaring their sexuality to family or friends.

> *...my mother said it was worse than a death in the family, my sister said she'd never known me, my brother sort of cut off from me.* (Gay and Grey in Dorset, 2006, p.51)

> *It wasn't received very well by my eldest son at all; in fact he didn't speak to me for two years...* (Gay and Grey in Dorset, 2006, p.51)

> *As you get older you like to talk of the past. In a heterosexual world this is a challenge and you find you constantly have to explain yourself. Older people become invisible* per se. (Gay and Grey in Dorset, 2006, p.35)

> *It's important to be in an environment where my cultural identity is understood.* (Gay and Grey in Dorset, 2006, p.30)

In his paper 'Assessing the cultural needs of older lesbians and gay men', Steve Pugh (2005) suggests that far from being a homogeneous community there are many differences both between and among lesbians and gay men. Due to alienation, family support has in many cases been replaced by friendships. This separates older lesbians and gay men from older people generally, who tend to receive support from relatives. Such alienation can result in lesbians and gay men being more alone in their later years. Where social policies are based on assumptions of heterosexual family units providing support and care, those cut off from their families are doubly isolated. *'No family/children to care or give company...'* (Gay and Grey in Dorset, 2006, p.35)

ACTIVITY 3

Identify any ways in which you consider the assessment process might be changed to ensure it is non-discriminatory and neither ageist nor heterosexist.

Think about how you elicit information and what you might be able to do to ensure that you are completely inclusive.

Think about and write down ways in which you might enable people to overcome their fears.

There are mixed views about the provision of exclusively lesbian or gay male residential/nursing homes (Gay and Grey in Dorset, 2006). Some consider that the only way of ensuring they are not isolated within a heterosexual world is to have such establishments. Others fear that this would lead to a ghetto culture and have no wish to live in circumstances which could also attract victimisation and create a target for homophobia. Heaphy and Yip (2006) note in their study that the preference for the majority is for lesbian- and gay-friendly and knowledgeable services and practitioners, rather than exclusive establishments. This was also the preference found by the Gay and Grey research (2006).

Pugh (2005) postulates that in the literature images of older lesbians and gay men are depicted very differently, with the former being portrayed as single or divorced with good education, professional employment and liberal policies; gay men, on the other hand, are stereotyped as being lonely, sad, depressed and sexual predators on young gay men who reject them. He speculates that these differences are influenced by the 'perceived lack of value of female sexuality and the threat of gay male sexuality' with gay men representing 'an assault to hegemonic masculinity' (p.208). However, the suggestion that older lesbians are more financially secure goes against the findings of Age Concern (2001), which found they were one of the poorest groups. Pugh also notes that Heaphy et al. (2003) 'reinforce previous findings around the significance and importance of friendship networks'. He goes on to state that the article identifies 'clear implications for the practice of health and social care professionals in their interaction with older lesbians and gay men' (p.216). He specifically lists the following:

- the hostility felt by older lesbians and gay men towards them expressed by health and social care professionals

- the lack of knowledge held by health and social care professionals about what it is to be lesbian or gay

- the need to acknowledge the diversity of experience and identity among older lesbians and gay men

- that such diversity should inform service provision

- that service provision should at least be demonstrably lesbian- and gay-friendly if not exclusively lesbian and gay

- that friendship networks, partners and children should be acknowledged with parity to heterosexual relationships. (p.216)

ACTIVITY 4

Either on your own or with a colleague, think about how your practice reflects this list and write down what changes you could make to ensure that you and your colleagues take them into everyday practice.

Write down ways in which you think you could help older lesbians and gay men express their needs.

Write down what you know about the history of older lesbians and gay men.

The cultural stereotypes of gay people being predatory or promiscuous, personal experience of discrimination, isolation from family, from a religious community and, in some instances, violence, all add to the desire on their part to withdraw and manage without outside help. This can exacerbate the effects of low income, poor diet, lack of exercise or social outlets and deteriorating health.

Structural

...the categories lesbian, gay, bisexual and straight are a reflection of our own society – they are of little relevance to many cultures...even to the UK before the mid-19th century. Sexuality is not a biological essence, unchanging through history...it is 'socially

constructed'. In many societies, gay men, lesbian women, bisexual and straight people simply do not exist. (Wilson, 2007, p.1)

Mid-nineteenth-century industrialisation led to marked changes in views on sexuality and morality. The movement of people from country to town resulted in overcrowding, which in turn created slums in which whole families frequently shared one room and, in many instances, shared one bed. This led to a situation where 'Capitalists were concerned that the working class was failing to reproduce itself, a possibility which threatened their wealth' (Wilson, 2007, p.4). Prior to this there was considerable tolerance of same-sex behaviour as is evidenced by such as the seventeenth and eighteenth-century 'molly houses' which were 'regular meeting places in which men drank and danced together, flirted with one another...and indulged in hugging, kissing and tickling each other as if they were a mixture of wanton males and females...' (Wilson, 2007, p.2). Also, in the eighteenth and early nineteenth centuries, women publicly formed 'passionate romantic friendships' (Wilson, 2007, p.3). Most famous were the two upper-class Irish women who eloped together in 1778 and settled in Wales where they shared every part of their lives for 53 years and became known as the Ladies of Llangollen (Wilson, 2007). Additionally, before the nineteenth century it was only the Church which had a problem with homosexuality in that it regarded sodomy as a punishable sin. According to Logan and Kershaw (1994), it was the developments in science and medicine that constructed homosexuality as 'unnatural', 'pathological', 'sick' and a threat to the family. This, together with the perceived threat to the wealth and position of capitalists, could be said to mean that the social construction of homosexuality became inevitable.

As age places people into a social position, so do heterosexism and homophobia. All three are based on stereotypes and misconceptions that have arisen from a society which places labels on those who don't conform to the accepted norm, are seen to lack power and influence or are perceived to threaten 'family values' and structures. Health and social care take place in a 'society dominated by a heterosexual hegemony which hates, fears, and is fascinated by lesbians and gay men' (Logan and Kershaw, 1994, p.62). The implications of assigning people can be far reaching and significantly affect their ability to change things. The lack of status, power and resources helps to perpetuate the existing social order, leading to further discrimination and marginalisation.

Alongside heterosexism and homophobia, the older lesbian and gay man also have to contend with ageism, the invisibility and assumptions of lack of ability and asexuality that seem to accompany ageing. According to Brown (1998, cited in Langley, 2001, p.917), old age is a social construction and is not in itself 'a reason for social work intervention'. Jack (1995, cited in Thompson and Thompson, 2001, p.62) makes the point that older people are:

- disempowered by poverty, poor housing, inadequate and discriminatory health and social services

- a diverse, heterogeneous group, despite often being treated as if representing a single homogeneous category

- regarded as a problem by service providers due to rising numbers and therefore rising overall costs

- prone to negative and debilitating stereotypes.

Add to this a complete disregard of, or open hostility to, their sexuality and therefore their life experiences and it is not surprising that many gay people view old age with fear and trepidation.

> *For closeted gays the problems around getting older are worse. Even if I didn't feel discriminated against I would feel the need to come out to every service provider...This requires emotional energy that I may not have if I become more frail.* (Gay and Grey in Dorset, 2006, p.36)

This possibility is recognised by Pugh (2005), who picks up Brown's (1998) comment about how continually coming out is exhausting. He states that someone who is being assessed may be unwell and need assistance. It is therefore expecting a great deal if they also have to 'engage in the exhausting process of coming out' (p. 215) and managing the potential reaction. Even people who consider that being open is important if progress is to be made can have reservations:

> *Although I think it is important to be open about my sexuality I still find it difficult. I do not like to have to make a public statement about an aspect of myself which is intensely personal.* (Gay and Grey in Dorset, 2006, p.20)

Many lesbians and gay men have lived most of their lives in fear of discovery, of being ostracised or persecuted because of their sexuality. For some that fear is based on personal experience of imprisonment, beatings, expulsion from family or community, loss of children or loss of livelihood. As they get older, that fear can be exacerbated by other fears:

> *In addition to the concerns of all people as they grow older – declining health, strength, independence – there is an increased risk of social and emotional isolation by belonging to a minority group in society.* (Gay and Grey in Dorset, 2006, p.34)

As was shown in the Gay and Grey (2006) research report being older, being gay, having physical impairments, ill health, disability, mental health problems, all contribute to a sense of isolation.

It must also be recognised that religions can marginalise gay people who, as a result, experience a double discrimination: an individual who has a religious belief that they feel unable to express because of their sexuality experiences great personal conflict in having to live two lies, and the impact of this conflict cannot be ignored. For some it can be as distressing as exclusion from the family:

> *I got talking to the local vicar and he said, 'Well of course we can't accept [gay] people in the Church'. Your sexuality is at the very heart of yourself, it is terribly dangerous to live a lie.* (Gay and Grey in Dorset, 2006, p.49)

While health and social care practitioners/providers maintain the structures of society by their language and behaviour, disempowerment and discrimination will continue. Openness to diversity of all kinds can result in a changing society which embraces everyone, including older heterosexual/asexual people as well as older lesbians and gay men:

> *...the ideal world is having a recognition that being lesbian or being gay is just part and parcel of the sexual continuum...we're all just ordinary human beings...* (Gay and Grey in Dorset, 2006, p.66)

The Department of Health (2006a) has produced 'Core Training Standards for Sexual Orientation' which states that it is essential that all staff, at all levels 'from porter to board room' are included in training. It also states that 'Changing heteronormative and hetero-centric patterns and behaviours that are associated with them is at best not easy and can be experienced as difficult, personally challenging and at times painful as old certainties have to be unlearned and new ways of doing things established. They can also be exciting and very rewarding'. (p.23)

In *Out of the Shadows*, Manthorpe and Price (2003) raise the issue of care for people with dementia and the dearth of practice-based evidence relating to older lesbians and gay men with mental health problems. It is not a subject that is within the remit of this chapter but it does need to be highlighted as an issue.

ACTIVITY 5

Write down the words that you and your colleagues/friends use to describe older lesbians and gay men or that you think describe them.

Identify the positive and negative words and see which is the greater.

What does that tell you about your attitudes? Do you think the results show that you have prejudices and misconceptions?

Can you think of ways in which negative stereotypes and misconceptions can be challenged/changed?

Think about and write down ways in which you might enable people to overcome their fears.

Conclusion

It is clear that attitudes have changed towards lesbians and gay men and that change is continuing. However, while there is some increase in public acceptance, the image of the ageing lesbian or gay man still all too frequently gives rise to jokes, hostility and harassment and the perpetuation of stereotypes. There also seems to be little recognition in literature, theatre or the media of the existence, needs and experiences of older lesbians and gay men. It can be disheartening to find that relatively little has changed despite the increasing amount of evidence and research into the experiences of older lesbians and gay men and the impact of heterosexism and homophobia.

For older lesbians and gay men, a lifetime of discrimination and fear can cause considerable difficulties. Faced with the assumption that heterosexuality is the norm, the lesbian or gay man must make a decision about whether or not to 'come out' and declare their sexuality or remain hidden. Such is the prevalence of 'heterosexism' that it might be necessary to make such a decision at each daily encounter. It needs more than legislation to ensure services are provided in an even-handed and inclusive way.

It is difficult to join in a conversation or interact with people whose lifetime experiences have been very different from yours or when you fear the reaction if you reveal a different sexuality. Also, if you have spent a lifetime finding ways to avoid declaring your sexuality it can become so innate that it is almost impossible not to continue. Fear of coming out can be so firmly rooted that it becomes a block for the individual. For some, to remain hidden is preferable to what might otherwise ensue. Thus, even an environment that is accepting and non-discriminatory may not enable disclosure and it is important that professionals respect an individual's decision not to 'come out'.

As Pugh (2005) has shown, it is essential that health and social care practice recognises the need to understand the individuality of older people, particularly older lesbians and gay men. Only when professionals recognise, respect and understand the differences can services start to meet individual needs. Practitioners must look to the ways in which they may be perpetuating stereotypes and, however unintentionally, contributing towards discrimination and the isolation of large numbers of older lesbians and gay men. By being open to diversity of experience and lifestyles of others, and challenging discriminatory views and practices, things can change for the better for everyone. A visual sign that sexual orientation is accepted and that lesbians and gay men are welcome is a good way to start developing trust. One simple way of doing this is to display the rainbow logo on all publications/leaflets/paperwork/correspondence. While that may be possible only in the long term (and may need local policy-decisions), a short-term step can be to place a sticker on the outside of file covers, diaries, etc., or even by wearing a badge.

People might be encouraged to declare their sexuality if asked in a straightforward, simple and jargon-free way, as suggested by Deborah Gold in 'Sexual exclusion issues and best practice in lesbian, gay and bisexual housing and homelessness' (2005, p.161). The example given is to ask 'How would you define your sexuality? Lesbian, gay, bisexual, heterosexual or unsure?' It is suggested that the term 'homosexual' should be avoided as it can seem formal and medical.

Working positively with older lesbians and gay men can be developed in the following ways:

- Accepting and acknowledging sexuality, individuality, experience and history.

- Recognising and acknowledging people's fears which may be based upon very real and unpleasant experiences.

- Demonstrating sensitivity and understanding of difference.

- Recognising and acknowledging the importance of individual support networks and relationships, both positive and negative.

- Respecting individual decisions not to 'come out', however clear their sexuality may appear to be to you.

- Recognising the right of the individual to have their basic needs met and to participate in social life.

- Fully involving users at all levels: planning, delivering and evaluating services.

- Looking upon users as partners and working with them towards agreed goals.

- Ensuring your language and actions are inclusive and non-discriminatory.

- Responding positively and treating seriously any indications of abuse, discrimination or harassment due to sexuality.

- Challenging homophobia and heterosexism in practice by:

  - keeping up to date with all appropriate policies and legislation

  - resisting the tendency to make assumptions and draw conclusions.

- Recognising and finding ways of overcoming your own prejudices and stereotypical assumptions.

- Never sharing the knowledge of someone's sexuality with anyone without their express agreement; just because they've told you doesn't mean they're comfortable about anyone else knowing.

- Learning something about lived experiences and non-heterosexual history.

Chapter 4
Promoting acceptance: visibility and validation

By Ann Fannin

Introduction

There is a body of evidence pointing to institutional homophobia in Britain and the wider world (McGhee, 2005) and a widespread, debilitating internalised homophobia within individual gay people (Williamson, 2000). As we shall see, in a society that is predominantly ageist and where people are less valued, less visible and more powerless as they get older, life becomes increasingly difficult for gay people in a particular way. For older black people, people from a minority culture or those with disabilities, the difficulty is accentuated. With fear of homophobia, actual or perceived, there is a temptation for some gay people to remain in or return to 'the closet' in old age (Gay and Grey in Dorset, 2006), thereby surrendering a major part of their identity at tremendous cost to their emotional well-being.

Over centuries, the ways in which lesbians and gay men have been accepted in a given society changed with the political, religious and social order of the day (Weeks, 1989; Wilson, 2007). More recently, with the decriminalisation of homosexuality in the 1970s and the passing of two significant pieces of legislation – the Civil Partnership Act (2004) and the Equality Act (2007) – the lives of some gay people, in Britain at least, are easier; a legal framework has been created in which to move forward. However, prejudice and discrimination still exist: overtly, covertly, institutionally and personally. 'Gay bashing' and homophobic bullying are still all too common (Stonewall, 2007a). Assumptions of heterosexuality can lead to the exclusion of gay people in many areas of social, medical, religious and political life. It is still deemed acceptable in some circles to make fun of gay people, demeaning them with stereotypical comments. Some comedians have dubious sketches portraying gay people in a derogatory way and, on a personal level, individuals still have to put up with jibes and jokes about their sexuality. The way the media portray homosexuality can accentuate the concept of difference by reinforcing stereotypes with negative imaging. As we have seen, many older lesbians, gay men or bisexual people are still wary of coming out to all people and live with anxiety on a daily basis as to whether they will be accepted (Gay and Grey, 2006). The rate of mental health problems among homosexual people is greater than those in the heterosexual population (King and McKeown, 2003), which highlights the problems gay people have to face. Our brief in this book is to focus on older lesbians and gay men; however, it is absolutely necessary to look at the situation surrounding all gay people before we can put them into a context.

It is estimated that between one in seven and one in ten of the population is gay (Stonewall, 2007b). The population of Britain is made up of almost 61 million people (National Statistics). Thus, well over 6 million of those will be lesbian or gay men. About 35 per cent of the whole population is over 50, which means that approximately 2.5–3 million of those will be older lesbians and gay men. Given that older lesbians and gay men are largely invisible in our society, there is concern that there is a significant number whose needs are not being met.

There is a great deal of work being done in many areas to combat homophobia and there is a lot of good practice in the community. In this chapter we shall look at some of this good practice and suggest further ways of promoting acceptance to make it easier for gay people to combat destructive internalised homophobia.

It is important at this stage to recognise that there are older gay people who live in such fear of exposure that they have never managed to identify themselves as lesbian, gay or bisexual to anyone. There are those whose life experiences or circumstances have dictated secrecy. Perhaps they have had to care for homophobic elderly parents, or lived in an isolated rural area where to come out would take enormous courage; maybe they have lived on an urban housing estate where homosexuality was not tolerated. Some of these older people may have had to suppress their sexuality for so long they no longer want to be found. Care must be taken to respect their privacy.

Socialisation has a powerful effect on human psychology and established ideas developed from childhood to adulthood are hard to break. To promote acceptance, challenge prejudice and move forward to an equitable society where all people are treated with equal respect, change is needed in all social, personal, cultural and political spheres. Changing attitudes, entrenched ideas and institutional practice are a complex business. Over the past 40 years, great strides have been made towards the liberation of homosexual people. Historically, for whatever reason, there have been disagreements and infighting within the gay community as to the way forward (Field, 1995). Each method has its own advantages and disadvantages, but there is no reason why any should be exclusive. In this chapter we shall look at some of the different ways in which people work and have worked towards a goal of liberation.

Activism: out of the closet

Collective political unity

The roots of the modern-day political struggle for gay emancipation is generally regarded to be embedded in the riots around the Stonewall Inn, a gay bar in Greenwich Village, downtown New York, in June/July of 1969 (Duberman, 1993). The riots in 1969 exploded out of systematic and brutal harassment by the police of lesbians, gay men, transvestites and transgender people who frequented the bar at that time. This was the touch-paper that sparked a mass movement throughout the United States of America, Europe and the United Kingdom and by the few coming out and demonstrating in a high-profile way, others found the confidence to join in the fight for justice and recognition. The movement consolidated with the formation of the Gay Liberation Front (GLF), which grew rapidly, spreading over America and culminating in a huge march to Central Park, New York, on 28 June 1970 (Knitting Circle, 2001).

By 1970, the resistance, encouraged by the general political atmosphere of the time and particularly influenced by the women's liberation movement, had spread to Britain. Branches of the GLF sprang up in local areas with radical political agendas and upfront protest actions (Field, 1995). The first organised protest march was in Highbury Fields London, on 27 November 1970, followed by another in August 1971. The first official Gay Pride march was held on 1 July 1972 with about 2,000 lesbians and gay men marching down Oxford Street to Hyde Park in Central London (Knitting Circle, 2001). A further 40,000 people marched in the Pride march of 1988 protesting against section 28 of the Local Government Bill 1988 forbidding 'promotion' of homosexuality in schools (Field, 1995). The Pride march in London has been held annually ever since. Others have been held in major cities throughout Great Britain. Recently, the focus of the annual march in London has changed to become a celebration, with the emphasis on fun rather than protest. Many business people have seen the day as an opportunity to make money, which has sadly excluded those who cannot afford to attend the now-ticketed festival.

Throughout the 1970s and 1980s, many lesbians and gay men, particularly in the early years among the GLF and other socialist groups like the Socialist Workers Party, actively involved themselves in political struggles and joined in workplace actions openly as gay people; probably the most famous example being unity with the striking miners in 1984–5, 'Lesbian and Gays Support the Miners' (LGSM). Chapters were formed throughout Britain and gay members marched side by side in solidarity with the strikers. In her book *Over the Rainbow*, Nicola Field (1995) describes how barriers and prejudices were broken down between the miners and lesbians and gay men by recognising similarities in their struggles and having open debates together on sex and sexuality. It also gave gay miners confidence to 'come out' themselves. Many miners and their families joined the Gay Pride march in 1985. As a direct result, the National Union of Miners led a campaign in 1985 to include sexual orientation in the equality policies of the Trades Union Congress. The issues of lesbian, bisexual and gay rights had moved forward in great strides and many other unions have now included sexual orientation in their policies of equality.

Individual actions

In the 1980s there was a number of memorable actions by daring individuals who wanted to highlight lesbian, gay and bisexual issues. On 18th February 1988, during a debate on section 28 of the Local Government Bill, two lesbians abseiled into the House of Lords, chanting slogans and waving banners. On 23 May 1988 those same women managed to get into the BBC newsroom and one handcuffed herself to Sue Lawley's chair as she read the headline news. Later they continued their protests by chaining themselves to the gates of Buckingham Palace (Cooper, 2003).

In the 1990s two controversial groups were founded: OutRage! and the Lesbian Avengers, both with policies of civil disobedience and non-violent direct action. These were imaginative, high profile, controversial and designed to catch the eye of the media for maximum publicity. Among a variety of protests, they staged a high profile 'Kiss In' at Piccadilly Circus in 1990 and they interrupted the Archbishop of Canterbury's Easter Sermon in 1998. In London they attempted a citizen's arrest of visiting Zimbabwe's President Robert Mugabe (1995) and they also disrupted an operatic performance of *Aida* at the Royal Albert Hall in 1996 (Tatchell, 1999). Many of their actions alienated and embarrassed some in the lesbian and gay community and some have been in danger of capitulating to racist ideas. However, these actions served to put established homophobic prejudice and discrimination high on the agenda with the aim of challenging the political order.

> *We pride ourselves in subverting the status quo and interrupting business-as-usual. It is precisely this unwillingness to conform to the rules of traditional political discourse that distinguishes our direct action politics from mainstream lobbyists.* (Tatchell, 1999)

'Mainstream lobbyists'

Several people who had been involved in the huge demonstration against section 28 of the Local Government Bill in 1988 were determined that laws should be challenged and attitudes changed in a more low-key and dedicated way. They wanted the anger generated from the anti-section 28 demonstrations put onto a more professional footing. Stonewall (which took its name from the inn in New York where the riots of the late 1960s had started) was subsequently founded in 1989.

Stonewall's main focus and aim was to lobby Parliament and work for change – particularly in legislation – within mainstream politics, and the members have courted all shades of opinion in Parliament and the House of Lords ever since. They have campaigned tirelessly and seen major successes over the years, including the repeal of section 28, the Civil Partnership Act and, most recently, the Equality Act. Stonewall became a charity in 2003 and is funded solely by donations, sponsorship and fund-raising by the membership which spans the width and breadth of Britain. In parallel to the lobbying of Parliament, they are now involved in research and information-gathering pertaining to lesbians, gay men and bisexuals. They have produced leaflets and designed web pages on subjects ranging from gay bullying in schools to safe sex, legal advice to homelessness, and parenting, to race issues. They also run a 'Diversity Champions' programme which involves liaising with and advising large and small businesses on lesbian, gay, bisexual and diversity issues (www.stonewall.org.uk). Stonewall has now become a respected and professional group of lobbyists and has done much to alter the lives of gay people.

Where are we now?

General view

It is now illegal to discriminate against lesbians, gay men and bisexual people in any way. Assaults that are motivated by prejudice on grounds of sexuality, race or disability are treated more harshly when a sentence is passed. Same-sex couples now have the right under the law to have a civil partnership, which affords them the same rights as those in a heterosexual marriage (albeit with different wording – a divorce is known as a 'dissolution' and a marriage is a 'civil partnership'). Lesbians, gay men and bisexuals are now able to join the armed services openly, same-sex couples can apply to adopt children and local authorities and other providers are obliged to offer goods and services to those in need without prejudice (see the Timeline on homosexuality and the law at the end of this book). Gay people themselves have driven this change, with Parliament responding to decades of dedicated campaigning. The scene is now set to move forward to a less prejudiced world.

Nevertheless, a great many issues still need to be confronted. Many people from all classes and creeds in Britain remain deeply homophobic. Institutional attitudes are largely heterosexual and heterosexuality is deemed to be the norm. There is still an alarming level of hate crime levelled at gay people. Studies have revealed that one in four lesbians had been the victim of homophobic violence during the period 1990–95 and one in three gay men (Stonewall, 2007b). Anecdotal stories within the gay community abound with tales of homophobic instances, and a fear of revealing oneself as gay is endemic (Gay and Grey in Dorset, 2006). Some feel that attitudes are more entrenched in rural areas than in the cities.

Many of the large institutions, local authorities, businesses and leisure industries have strong and positive equality statements – including sexual orientation – enshrined in their policies. However, disadvantaged people, from all areas of life, experience discrimination in very specific ways and it is important to understand each perspective and deal with each individually. Many organisations have equality and diversity statements but do not follow through with specific training on lesbian, gay, bisexual and transgender (LGBT) issues. Appropriate training must therefore go hand-in-hand with the relevant policy statements.

Moving towards equality: what progress has been made?

Education and schools

Many of the interviewees in the Gay and Grey research project identified their school years in the 1930s, 1940s and 1950s as being particularly difficult in terms of homophobic bullying and harassment. Today, although there have been no national surveys on homophobic bullying recently, there have been several surveys locally in the UK, the USA and Australia. These have routinely shown that between 30 per cent and 50 per cent of young people in education have experienced some form of homophobic bullying (Warwick et al., 2004).

It is not within the remit of this chapter to research how the repeal of section 28 (which prohibited the 'promotion' of homosexuality in schools and local government) has affected the curriculum or attitudes in schools, although it appears that little research

Work needs to be placed in a wider context where lesbians, gay men and bisexuals are seen as citizens and participants in a wide range of activitites.
(NUT, 2004)

has been done to find out. The National Union of Teachers (NUT, 2004) suggests that schools should use the curriculum to promote awareness by making links not only in subjects like citizenship and specific awareness sessions, but within art, English, drama and history where issues of stereotypes and gay prejudice could be explored. It is important to provide positive images of lesbian, gay and bisexual people; information on famous homosexual people from both past and present could easily and naturally be included in the day-to-day lessons and lectures.

Among lesbian and gay teachers there is a reluctance to talk publicly about the situation in their particular school or college, which is indicative of a general nervousness about gay issues within the profession. In their research, Warwick et al. (2004) found that 'Teachers are said to be the occupational group who find it most difficult to be open about their sexuality in the work place' (p.20). To push things forward, each school should not only have robust equality and diversity policies, but should involve everybody – pupils, governors, parents, management and teaching staff – in developing a culture of same-sex acceptance and validity. With the new legal responsibilities to challenge prejudice and discrimination, schools now have to take the issue seriously. What is needed is a 'whole school approach' (NUT, 2004) where everyone in a particular school is not only aware of the issues but will act positively to eradicate homophobia.

Strides have been made in schools and colleges. In some sixth-form colleges, lesbian, gay and bisexual groups have been established and many schools have tight policies on homophobic bullying. Good practice appears patchy and in the absence of firm research it is difficult to quantify. The nearest we can get is a quote from Ofsted, the watchdog on standards in schools:

> *In too many secondary schools homophobic attitudes among pupils often go unchallenged. The problem is compounded when derogatory terms about homosexuality are used in everyday language and their use passes unchallenged by staff. Where these problems arise, staff have often had insufficient guidance on the interpretation of school values and what constitutes unacceptable language or behaviour.* (Ofsted cited in NUT, 2004, p.3)

Churches

During the Gay and Grey (2006) research project, people talked of either having been rejected by the Church or of being afraid to 'come out' to people in the congregation for fear of rejection:

> *I do avoid situations where religion is concerned, because people can get very heated about that and tell you that you're going to hell.* (Gay and Grey in Dorset, 2006, pp. 49–50)

Some denominations – the Roman Catholic Church for instance – forbid the taking of sacraments to those who are practising homosexuals. This can be painful for gay people who have been brought up in the faith; it can cause considerable pain not to be accepted and is the cause of much guilt and self-doubt.

The Roman Catholic Church regards same-sex relationships as a 'serious depravity'. However, they say, 'This judgment of Scripture does not of course permit us to conclude that all those who suffer from this anomaly are personally responsible for it, but it does attest to the fact that homosexual acts are intrinsically disordered' (www.vatican.va/roman_congregation/cfaith). The Catholic Church is not alone in these ideas. Other religions like the Evangelical Christians, the Methodists, the Free Presbyterians, Fundamentalist Muslims, Salvation Army and many others share the Catholic Church's belief that homosexuality is either sinful or against the natural order of things. With the Anglican Church of England and others split for and against gay support, life can be difficult for the faithful. The reactionary stance of many religions is a further negative factor in gay people's lives, undermining their self-esteem and forcing them to lead secret lives of fear and internalised shame.

There are, however, churches that are much more open and welcoming to everyone, whatever their sexuality. The Quakers, the Metropolitan Community Church (MCC) and the Open Episcopal Church offer an open door to all.

> *A lot of gay and lesbian people have, in the past, been made to feel that they are not acceptable to God. The more gay and lesbian people know there are Churches who will tell them God loves them, the better.* (Personal communication from Bishop Stewart Harrison of the Open Episcopal Church)

One interviewee in the Gay and Grey (2006) research project, who had been brought up as a Christian, wanted to be ordained but, as he explained, *'I got talking to the local vicar and he said well of course we can't accept gay people in the Church'* (p.50). Later he joined the MCC, which was much more accepting:

> *I found it very good that I could just be myself; I could do what I wanted to do, come to church, enjoy church...I could be openly gay amongst people here, even straight people who are coming to church, just accepting me and I thought, wow this is good.* (Gay and Grey in Dorset, 2006, p.50)

Police

In the past few years, many of the police forces in Britain have started to take homophobic hate crime very seriously. A total of 23 different police forces have joined together to provide an information pack (True Vision: www.report-it.org.uk) in conjunction with Stonewall, Age Concern and the Crown Prosecution Service. This pack provides advice on homophobic hate crime and domestic violence and copies have been distributed widely in pubs, clubs, libraries and health groups. Many forces across Britain have also created liaison officers within the service, aiming to break down old suspicions of the police and to encourage people to come forward to report hate crime. Progress nationally appears patchy but in many areas lesbian and gay liaison officers (LAGLO) are working with the gay community with some success.

Inspector Shaun Cronin of the Partnership and Diversity Development Team, Dorset Police, said

> *LAGLO in Dorset was formed eight years ago and was regarded then as very forward-thinking. Until now we have effectively managed on good will and enthusiasm; there has*

been no National Standard to conform to; however this may change soon...The aim of LAGLO is to recognise and liaise with the gay community – we are not here to judge but to present a professional friendly face and to encourage people to report homophobic hate crime. Traditionally the police have not been trusted. We now engage with the gay community and have regular liaison meetings. In Bournemouth with its large gay community it is easy to engage with them, it is not so easy in the rural areas; this is reflected nationwide.' (Personal communication with Inspector Shaun Cronin)

A homophobic incident is one which is perceived to be homophobic by the victim or any other person. (Dorset LAGLO, 2007)

This kind of project can only improve the situation for all lesbians and gay men, young and old. Suspicion of the police is hard to break, particularly for those who experienced harsh homophobic treatment during years of draconian anti-homosexual laws; but there are signs of improvement and more homosexual hate crimes are being reported. To date, there do not appear to be firm statistics, but anecdotal reports from individual police officers confirm that LGBT people are more confident in reporting homophobia hate crime than they were a decade ago. The relaxing of attitudes towards gay people has also had an effect within the police forces and has given confidence to lesbian and gay police to come out themselves. Some join in Gay Pride marches openly in uniform, with the support of their particular force, while others are refused permission. A National Gay Police Association (www.gay.police.uk) has now been established with the aim of supporting lesbian and gay police service employees, with several local forces affiliating to it. Progress is being made.

The force is more tolerant now than it was, but it has yet to reach the next level – acceptance – which is to value what gay officers bring to the service. (Vic Coding, *BBC News 24*, 30 September 2004)

The media

In many ways, the media reflect the society in which we live, but it can be a powerful tool for change. For many years television has tended to reinforce the idea of a standard stereotype in their portrayal of lesbian, gay men, bisexuals and transgender people. There have been very few role models for gay people to relate to. If gay people have been used on TV they have tended to be game-show hosts, or in comedy reviews making demeaning 'jokes' with the clichéd limp wrist and dyed hair. Stonewall, in recent research, monitored 168 hours of peak time viewing on BBC 1 and BBC 2; only six minutes were deemed satisfactory in portraying lesbian and gay people positively. Gay people and their lives are five times more likely to be portrayed in negative terms on the BBC (Stonewall, 2007b).

I think that if everbody in public life who was gay or lesbian came out, that would help. I think laws that are enforced against discrimination in housing, work etc. would help, but it's the climate of opinion that needs changing – that's tricky. (Interviewee, Gay and Grey in Dorset, 2006, p.52)

Gradually, though, change is happening. Ordinary gay and lesbian couples are occasionally used on programmes like *Cash in the Attic*, *A place in the Sun*, and *Changing Rooms*. The gentler afternoon soap opera, *Doctors*, has recently portrayed a gay doctor's life appropriately for several episodes. *Dr Who*, the popular science fiction series, now has a gay character to whom children and others can relate. And gay couples are sometimes seen in billboard and television advertisements. As yet there have been no programmes which deal with or portray older lesbians or gay men, however; they remain invisible. Positive role models are important, not only for lesbians and gay men themselves but for general awareness, to learn more about lesbian and gay lives, and to recognise that homosexual people are little different from heterosexuals; that all humankind has more in common than their differences.

The Civil Partnership Act (December 2004)

Civil partnership registration underlines the inherent value of committed same-sex relationships. It supports stable families and shows that we really respect the diversity of the society we live in. It opens the way to respect, recognition and justice for those who have been denied it too long. (Jaqui Smith MP, Minister for Equality, June 2003)

This Act provided impetus towards equality and validation for lesbians and gay men.

The legal recognition of same-sex love and commitment has given confidence to lesbians and gay men – including many older couples who had been in long-term relationships – to publicly declare their love for each other. Many are eager to celebrate openly in mainstream hotels, restaurants and leisure outlets. Businesses have begun to see the potential of 'the pink pound' and many are more than willing to offer civil partnership ceremonies and receptions, goods and services. Anecdotal stories are told of couples being 'amazed' by the warmth and friendliness which surround them on 'coming out' to all those involved in their same-sex celebrations. Equally, those heterosexuals who have been involved in organising and servicing civil partnerships have been moved and touched by the experience, treating each couple with equal respect.

Equality Act (Sexual Orientation) Regulations 2007

With the passing of the Equality Act (Sexual Orientation) Regulations 2007, it is now against the law to exclude gay people from any goods or services. Consequently, more gay people are seen openly in public places; it is no longer necessary for them to hide their sexuality in terms of the law. This is a positive move forwards. It means, for instance, that gay people can now book a double bed in a hotel without fear of refusal and they can be more open in their leisure pursuits by joining mainstream facilities.

If we are accepted as legal and our partnership is validated in the eyes of the law, then I can hold my head up high and not care what everyone else thinks; this Act has been the biggest confidence-booster of my life and people are now accepting me for who I am.' (Volunteer, with the Gay and Grey group in Dorset, 2006)

Where do we go from here?

The situation we are in is problematic. There have been great strides made towards equality. The twentieth and twenty-first centuries have seen massive changes in attitudes towards lesbian and gay people. Laws have gradually relaxed through the years and now, finally, it is illegal to discriminate against homosexuals in any way. But there are still institutions, particularly within many religious communities, that remain steeped in dogma and reactionary ideas.

Changing heteronormative and heterocentric patterns and the patterns of behaviours that are associated with them, is at best not easy and can be experienced as difficult, personally challenging and at times painful as old certainties have to be unlearned and new ways of doing things established. They can also be exciting and very rewarding.
(Cree and O'Cora, 2006, p.24)

Attitudes, in some instances, have lagged behind the law. Prejudice and homophobia still linger in the corners of people's minds. Personal internalised homophobia is debilitating and the majority of lesbians and gay men remain fearful of revealing their sexuality. Prejudice in society is difficult to eradicate and, as gay people are largely invisible, particularly the old, it is easy to either ignore the issue or to absorb reactionary ideas. Both combating internalised homophobia and promoting acceptance in society is intrinsically and circularly linked. If more lesbians and gay men felt able to come out publicly as gay, it would become normal for the wider community to know homosexual people. However, for gay people to feel easy in coming out, there has to be a safe and friendly environment in which to be 'out' in.

Confidence-building and empowerment: public acceptance

There is much work to be done in the community and on personal levels to reassure lesbians and gay men that they have a safe environment in which to be themselves. There are some fine examples of intent. The Greater London Authority (2006), for instance, has been the vanguard with its Sexual Orientation Equality Scheme in which they formulate an action plan towards sexual orientation equality. This document, the first of its kind in Britain, is unequivocal in its statement of intent to work with all agencies, including MPs, stakeholders in the National Health Service, the forces of law, unions, business, education, housing leisure and all policy-makers, to ensure inclusion and visibility of the lesbian, gay and bisexual communities. The Greater London Authority has had a fine tradition in working towards lesbian and gay equality and has, for many years, worked tirelessly in championing gay rights, particularly within employment and in tackling homophobic attitudes. However, as they say, 'Service provision does not reflect this position' (Greater London Authority, 2006, p.7); theory is always easier than practice.

The Citizens Advice Bureau (CAB) is another example of open and good practice. They require all their Bureaux to display prominently a poster clearly defining their commitment to the gay community. Staff and volunteers are also required to attend diversity awareness training. The CAB is taking positive steps towards relating to the lesbian and gay community.

- We challenge all forms of discrimination, prejudice and harassment against lesbians, gay men and bisexuals.

- We are an equal opportunity employer and seek involvement as lesbians, gay men and bisexuals in the CAB service.

- We are independent and give free confidential advice to everyone who needs it regardless of sexuality, race and gender or disability.

- We provide advice that meets the needs of lebians, gay men and bisexuals and we work to influence local and national policies which may affect them. (2006)

(Affirmation towards gay people; wording from a poster which hangs in many CAB offices throughout the country)

'All local branches are autonomous, but must follow National Guidelines...We are aware that we are not perfect...in reality there is still fear, particularly for the older gay person...we, in Bournemouth are pretty good but could be better when dealing with older lesbians, gay men and bisexuals...in reality even in our open organisation, living up to our policies has proved difficult...particularly in the rural areas. (Personal communication from Martin Broad, Bournemouth CAB and co-chair of the National LGB CAB group)

Confidence-building to combat internalised homophobia

Gay people need to play an equal part by confronting their own internalised homophobia and personal fear. Combating internalised homophobia assimilated over years is very hard; for some it is impossible. Entrenched homophobic attitudes are not easy to shift. It is a two-way process. Everyone needs to work together for change.

There is no doubt that it is easier for some to come out than others. The more isolated the person, the harder it is; support is crucial. What are the issues?

- The importance of social groups for lesbians and gay men. This was highlighted in the Gay and Grey report (2006, pp.42–3). For older people, particularly in rural areas, the problem of isolation is more acute. Traditional gay venues – pubs and clubs – are invariably youth- and alcohol-orientated, which older people tend not to want. The existence of groups specifically for older lesbians and gay men is patchy throughout Britain, particularly for gay men. The development of social clubs should be a priority for local authorities and voluntary bodies. This could be integrated in community development work, particularly with local older gay people.

- Collective action is empowering and builds personal confidence. Anecdotally, there is evidence that gay men and women develop enormous confidence after going to their first Pride marches. In some towns like Brighton and Manchester the whole community gets involved with these festivals regardless of their sexuality.

- Solidarity and acceptance in the workplace and community. Public actions with others have proved life-enhancing. This encourages interaction and understanding between heterosexuals and homosexuals, and breaks down barriers. Everyone needs the support of others.

- Role models are important. Recognition that there are many other lesbians and gays, old and young, of all classes, creeds and cultures throughout the world is inspiring.

- Positive messages for gay people in public places can boost self-esteem; a higher profile in the community is a priority. Information leaflets and posters could be placed in all public places, hospitals, tourist information offices, doctors' surgeries, libraries, supermarkets and council offices. The messages need to be loud and clear: that older lesbians and gay men are a valued part of society.

- Understanding that homosexuality is normal and regarded generally as valid is self-affirming; information and positive propaganda should be widespread.

- A safe environment is crucial for gay people to enable them to be 'out and proud' in their communities; homophobic hate and prejudice must be challenged and visibility encouraged.

Training and awareness for practitioners who work with older people

Working with diversity seeks to focus on the strengths and positives of difference, as well as the problems; engages with and understands the totality of people's identity and experience; and recognises and confronts experiences of oppression and discrimination and their impact on the individual. (Tegg, 2006, p.9)

One of the priorities emerging from the Gay and Grey (2006) research project was a need to support and develop awareness programmes, with training specifically on sexual orientation and homosexuality. There is a widespread assumption of heterosexuality throughout society and this needs to be challenged. Homophobia is not necessarily knowingly malicious and can stem from ignorance, but if it is not eradicated gay people will remain isolated and fearful. The whole of society needs to become involved and to learn just what the issues are. For those who are working with older people it is important to treat each person as an individual and to be aware of difference.

There clearly is a commitment from many official bodies, in the private, the public and the voluntary sectors, towards a more equitable and diverse society with robust training programmes in place.

> *Our mandate is to build a safe, just and tolerant society for everyone in the UK, regardless of their race, religion, gender, gender identity, sexual orientation, disability or age. (Home Office, 2007)*

However, what appears to be happening is the development of all-embracing, 'one size fits all' training packages. That is, a model, for example, which takes in concepts of a many-stranded discrimination; recognising that prejudice and power used negatively to justify actions can perpetuate any oppression, while non-hierarchical anti-discriminatory practice which uses power positively, can be empowering to all (Southampton City Council, 2007). This type of model works on the premise that, if truly working in anti-discriminatory ways, i.e. 'working with the whole person and the richness of their diversity'

(Tegg, 2006, p. 9), then acceptance and recognition of experienced oppression will automatically be perceived and understood within general standards of good practice. Of course, every individual's experiences are different and the whole person does need to be 'engaged with', but repression emanating from homophobia, either internalised or externalised, can be deep and remain unexplored unless there is an awareness of this distinct form of repression which is dealt with specifically.

- Discrimination in diversity can be multifaceted. Many of us cannot be defined by one strand of diversity. However, homosexuality in itself is not visible (as is a physical disability or skin colour) and is more difficult to identify.

- Most older lesbians and gay men have lived their lives with threats of homophobic discrimination and hostility, and a high percentage feel unable to reveal their sexuality to everyone (Gay and Grey in Dorset, 2006). Many have lived with a cult of secrecy and fear for most of their lives and many become invisible in the community. To come out in later life and accept that a major part of one's life has been given to living a lie (out of necessity) is extremely hard.

- Older lesbians and gay men have experiences in common with all older people: older people *per se* are deemed to be asexual and are generally marginalised. For older lesbians and gay men, the marginalisation goes much deeper with their sexuality unrecognised. With a global assumption of heterosexuality, the needs of homosexuals are overridden if not recognised. Many approaches by practitioners can be inappropriate and isolating (Gay and Grey in Dorset, 2006).

Conclusion

If equality and diversity are shown to be top level priorities, the likelihood of them being translated into action is high. (Cree and O'Cora, 2006, p.38)

When looking at the issues of older lesbians and gay men, it is necessary to not only see them in the context of generalised homophobia, but also in the context of a divided society. The road to equality is long and hard and the complexities of personal dynamics and wider politics are intricate and interwoven. For decades, lesbians, gay men and bisexuals have led the way in the struggle against discrimination, and the time is now right for all people to ensure that the gains made over the years are not lost and that homophobia is made a thing of the past. Laws are now on the statute books to make discrimination against lesbians, gay men and bisexuals illegal. Policy statements are firmly in place, but to be meaningful these have to be followed up with positive action by changing entrenched attitudes in all strands of society. Policy statements can only be the scaffolding from which to build equality.

Laws challenging racism and sexism have been in place for many years, but equality still eludes us, as lesbian or gay people. Black people or people from ethnic minorities remain prone to racist attacks and discrimination in many forms. The position of women in society is still unequal to that of men. People with disabilities remain marginalised. There are many forms of prejudice and inequality; for working-class people these disadvantages and discriminations hit hardest. Diversity and equality are now high on the agenda (HMSO, 2006) and staff training is seen as a priority in many government departments. However, there is evidence that some people feel there is a 'hierarchy between the diversity strands with sexual orientation holding a lower rank' (Cree and O'Corra, 2006, p.15). It is important that this is challenged and that sexual orientation awareness is given equal status with all threads of diversity.

This text has been designed to focus on homosexuality and specifically on how homophobia impacts on older lesbians and gay men. For those working as practitioners with older people there are many issues for them to take into account regarding diversity and sexual orientation.

Issues for each practitioner to reflect on

- Their awareness in relation to sexuality, prejudice and oppression and to the impact that homophobia has on older lesbians, gay men and bisexuals.

- How much knowledge they have about recent legislation which outlaws homophobic discrimination and about the implications these laws have on their own practice.

- In what ways they can challenge heterosexual assumptions when working with older people and develop an understanding of how these assumptions operate in the community.

- The importance of sensitivity towards those who do not feel confident to disclose their sexuality and indeed towards those who do.

- How to include all staff in discussions at workplace-level about issues associated with diversity in later life and sexuality.

- Developing an awareness of their own attitudes and prejudices concerning homosexuality.

- Becoming responsible for their own positive use of power to:

  - empower gay people themselves to develop their self-esteem

  - change attitudes of colleagues and build for a service which promotes inclusion, self-expression, and specific individual needs of lesbians and gay men.

It is sometimes said, that the days of discrimination are over for gay people, and that they should just put their heads down and get on with life. It is true that the situation has eased in Britain and legally there is equality and protection from overt homophobia. However, assumptions and attitudes are more difficult to shift. As we have seen, there are still unacceptable levels of homophobic attacks in society, and prejudices still can cling in the dark shadows of people's minds. The assumed culture of heterosexuality is widespread and all-embracing. Understanding the special circumstances of older lesbians and gay men is the key to good practice for practitioners and each individual has to play their part in the challenge to make homophobia – in whatever form – a thing of the past.

Chapter 5
Care settings and the home

By Nichola Lavin

Introduction

This chapter considers older lesbians and gay men in relation to care settings and the home. It argues that the personal and social aspects of 'home' which the service user identifies as important need to be considered and preferably recreated in care settings. The chapter will also highlight and discuss some of the concerns older gay people raise when faced with the prospect of entering supported accommodation, which professionals will need to take into account in their assessment. The chapter is arranged into three sections: the first section will present theories relating to the necessary elements of a home, along with a discussion of how this could apply to the placement of older lesbians and gay men. The second section will discuss issues relating to older lesbians and gay men entering care settings, as identified by service users, with the final section highlighting issues pertaining to home care. Several opportunities for reflection will be provided throughout.

The chapter is written under two premises, which need to be taken into account in your reading. The first is that older lesbians and gay men, while sharing much in common with the older population in general, do have specific concerns that require consideration. Pugh (2005) suggests that 'these differences should be taken into account in the assessment process, and in turn should influence service provision' (p.207). These 'differences' were highlighted by one of the questionnaire respondents in the 'Lifting the Lid' project (Gay and Grey, 2006):

> *In addition to the concerns of all people as they grow older – declining health, strength, independence – there is an increased risk of social and emotional isolation by belonging to a minority group in society.* (p.34)

The second premise is that every older lesbian and gay man experiences their sexuality as uniquely as they do ageing (Pugh, 2005). While this may seem obvious, there can be a tendency when talking about minorities to group them together into one homogenous population, because of their shared concerns. With this in mind, it is important to note that the development and expression of sexual identity will vary enormously between individuals, reflecting diversity of experience. As such, Hughes (2003) suggests that professionals need to be acutely aware of variations in the 'meaning different people give to their sexual identity and how it is expressed in their lives', and recognise that this meaning 'may differ from that which society gives it' (p.262). It follows, therefore, that any support given, or options highlighted, need to be considered within 'the context of the particular needs, vulnerabilities and strengths of older lesbian women and gay men' (Langley, 2001, p.917).

There's no place like home

For many of us our 'home', the space we live in, is of central importance in our lives. In Western cultures, the home is generally presented as a safe place where we can close the door and shut out the world, providing a sanctuary and a space to be whoever we choose to be. This is borne out by popular statements such as 'at home', which expresses a certain ease and comfort, and 'home is where the heart is', a place we hold in affection (www.askoxford.com). As we grow older, it's also a place of accumulated personal belongings and memories, perhaps of the times we shared with loved ones, friends and family, with the specific age-related value of home to older people being shown to have particular significance (Tanner, 2003). Given this, along with the desire to remain independent and retain some degree of control over our lives, it is no surprise that the majority of older people choose to stay in their homes as long as possible.

Duncan and Lambert (2004, cited in Waitt and Gorman-Murray, 2007) indicate that our homes are also important for identity construction, acting as 'primary sites in which identities are produced and performed in practical, material and repetitively affirming ways' (p.1). Furthermore, Annison (2000) indicates that the 'the creation and experience of home is an important contributor to a person's humanity and their positive social perception by others' (p.251). This suggests that 'not only is it a place, but it has psychological resonance and social meaning' (Saegert, 1985, cited in Annison, 2000, p.254). The home may also have additional significance for gay people, whose identities can be inhibited in everyday life (Gorman-Murray, 2006).

Given that the home is clearly significant in terms of individual identity and social meaning, importance should be attached to sheltered accommodation, residential care and home-care providers replicating and maintaining 'the home' in their care settings; and not just for gay people, but for all service users who require supported accommodation. This is reflected in government policy on residential care (Centre for Policy and Ageing, 1996; DoH, 1989) and is supported by Annison (2000), who recommends that any 'consideration of community living arrangements as they affect people in societally devalued groups, should also examine the nature of home because of the central role of "the home" in contributing to high quality community living' (p.252).

So what are the important aspects of 'home' that care settings should be trying to replicate? The question of what makes a home has been explored across various disciplines and for the purposes of this chapter I have selected three theories which illustrate the mechanisms that turn a place of residence into a home. This is followed by a discussion suggesting how these theories may be applicable to older lesbians and gay men.

Models of home

Sixsmith (1986) devised a model which distinguishes the home from other environments. The model highlights the three important elements of a home as personal, social and physical (Table 1). For each of these elements a list of descriptors shows how a home could be experienced by the individual; for example, a home is a place where individuals experience a sense of belonging, or a place where they can express themselves.

Personal	Happiness	Experience of happy events
	Belonging	Comfort, relaxation, familiarity
	Responsibility	Stability arising from ownership and responsibility
	Self-expression	Behaviour and manipulation of space
	Critical experiences	Learning independence, formative experiences
	Permanence	Continuity
	Privacy	Control of interpersonal world
	Time perspective	Home exists whether in the past, present or future
	Meaningful places	Specific events took place there
	Knowledge	Familiarity – physical and social knowledge
	Preference to return	A locus in space
Social	Type of relationship	Personal choice, being with particular people
	Quality of relationships	Acceptance in relationships
	Friends and entertainment	People visiting
	Emotional environment	A place of love often signifies home
Physical	Physical structures	Enduring physical characteristics
	Extent of services	Lighting, heating, garden, etc.
	Architectural style	
	Work environment	
	Spatiality	Activities that space allows

Table 1 Sixsmith (1986, p.287) Categories of home

Smith (1994) similarly described the home as a 'complex multi-dimensional concept, which is experienced simultaneously as a physical environment, a social environment and a place for the satisfaction of personal needs'(p.31), seeing the 'act of dwelling' as 'an integral part of human experience' with the home being 'a significant place for most people' (p.33). From this work emerged a list of the essential contributors to a sense of home (Table 2).

Physical	Social	Personal
Physical features Location Aesthetics	Positive social relationships: internal and external	Atmosphere Comfort Self-expression Freedom/control of space Privacy Personalisation, favourite possessions Ownership Shelter/security/safety Pride/achievement Relaxation

Table 2 Smith (1994, p.36) Contributors to sense of home

The opposite of these factors are contributors to environments that are not considered to be homes; for example, lack of personal freedom and privacy, dissatisfaction with social relationships, poor physical environment, negative atmosphere, etc.

Depres (1991, p.100) discusses differing approaches to the meaning of home, including a psycho-analytical approach which 'defines the home as a symbol of one's self', and a socio-psychological approach in which 'the home plays a crucial role in people's definition of their self-identity, acting as a dialogue between them and the larger community' as well as an 'important symbol of individuals' social identity' (1991, p.101). She also discusses a psychological approach, utilising Maslow's theory of personality (1954), which suggests that the home enables individuals to achieve psychological well-being through providing 'a shelter answering human need for physical security and health' (p100).

Depres (1991) suggests 10 categories that encompass the meaning of home, as identified by its occupants (Table 3).

Home as security and control Home as a reflection of one's ideas and values Home as acting upon and modifying one's dwelling Home as permanence and continuity Home as relationships with family and friends Home as centre of activities Home as a refuge from the outside world Home as an indicator of personal status Home as material structure Home as a place to own	Feelings of physical security How people see themselves and want to be seen by others Achievement, self-expression, freedom of action Familiarity, memories, sense of belonging Emotional experiences, acceptance Pastimes, eating, etc. Sanctuary, privacy and independence Socio-economic position Physical attributes, neighbourhood Freedom, permanence, pride

Table 3 Depres (1991, p.97) Categories of meaning of home

As a basic requirement, it is assumed that care settings can fulfil the attributes of a suitable physical environment, as highlighted by the above; that is, architecture, provision of heating and lighting, material structure, etc. What is argued in this chapter relates more specifically to the personal and social aspects of home.

To illustrate how these theories may be applicable to older lesbians and gay men, please consider the following example and reflect on the points below. This is followed by a discussion.

> *Harold is a gay man in his 80s who lives in a rural village. He is not 'out' to neighbours or any but his closest friends (who are also predominantly older gay men). In conversation, Harold is always careful not to disclose information about himself, which might lead others to suspect he is gay. He fears that if others knew of his sexuality he would be in danger, to the point where he is often visibly anxious. He lives alone and has no family support. He prefers not to socialise in public places with his gay friends for fear that conversations will be overheard and that this will lead to homophobic abuse.*

REFLECTION

a) *Can you think why 'the home' might be of particular importance to Harold (above and beyond the physical attributes) in his current situation?*

b) *If Harold gets to the stage where he is unable to live at home independently, what special considerations would an assessment need to take into account regarding his lifestyles? Which aspects of his current home life do you think would be under threat?*

Discussion

a) Here, the home could be of particular importance to Harold at both a personal and a social level.

Home as a personal space

Depres (1991), Smith (1994) and Sixsmith (1986) all highlight the importance of self-expression in a home, and for Harold, his home is among the very few places where he where he feels he can be absolutely himself. This view is supported by Gorman-Murray's (2006) research, which highlights the value of homes to gay people as private places where they can express themselves. At home, Harold is able to express his identity and his sexuality through items such as books, magazines and films, and because he has control over who enters into his environment he has no fear that others will be able to see them.

The home also offers Harold privacy, which again was cited by the three theorists as a contributor to what makes a home. Young (2004, cited in Gorman-Murray, 2006, p.151) argues that privacy is vital 'for enacting and materialising personal identity at home', defining privacy as 'the autonomy and control a person has to allow or not allow access to her person, information about her, and the things that are meaningfully associated with her person'. Harold can invite gay friends or lovers over, have privacy and talk freely without worrying that others can overhear or make judgements. Harold's home is a place where he is able to relax, be comfortable and be accepted for who he is. The home is his safe space and, I would argue, a vital space for maintaining his mental health.

55

Home as a social space

All three of the theories of home I have mentioned have included a social aspect, referring to the relationships we have with other people and the quality of those relationships. Accepting that socialising with others promotes well-being, particularly for older people, for older lesbians and gay men the opportunity to meet and socialise with other older lesbians and gay men (or of course younger lesbians and gay men), if not in the home, may otherwise be limited.

Socialising in homes can be particularly important for older lesbians and gay men, who traditionally formed social groups which met behind closed doors in people's homes – due to a lack of alternatives in many places, the law against homosexuality until the late 1960s, and more generally to avoid the heterosexual gaze. Many of these groups continue to run today, particularly in communities where other options remain unavailable, or just as an alternative to the 'gay scene' with its pubs and clubs, which may offer little of interest to some older people. These groups can offer positive affirmation and acceptance and have the potential to help people overcome isolation (particularly in more rural areas), with many offering social events in member's homes involving activities such as book clubs, barbecues and parties. They can also provide a secure and private place for people to meet like-minded individuals. This has been borne out by Gorman-Murray (2006), who suggests that some gay men and lesbians continue to use their homes to 'validate sexual difference...by using their home as a socialising space' (p.147). He suggests that by creating lesbian and gay communities within domestic settings, homes can generate and affirm lesbian and gay identities.

Furthermore, as the 'performance of same-sex intimacy remains socially proscribed in streets, parks, restaurants, work places and shopping centres' (Gorman-Murray, 2006, p.146), for older gay people, the home remains one of the few places where it is acceptable to openly show affection. As such, the home becomes 'crucial for developing intimate relations between partners' (Gorman-Murray, 2006, p.146) and, as Sixsmith (1986) suggests, a place of love often signifies a home.

b) In making an assessment of the most appropriate care setting for Harold, I would want to consider how the personal and social aspects of home would be met. How could I ensure, for example, that Harold would feel accepted for who he is in a residential care setting? How could I ensure that he feels safe to express his sexuality and feels comfortable enough to be open with staff and other residents, particularly when he is so fearful of being open? How could I ensure that he has continuing control over his environment and that he is exposed to positive opportunities to develop and maintain quality relationships – that wherever he is based he feels a sense of belonging and acceptance? These are issues which will be considered in more detail in the next section.

Summary

In this section I have stated that the home is an important space, highlighting theories which specify the important aspects of home as being a personal space, a social space and a physical space. Experiencing the home in these ways contributes to having positive relationships and a strong sense of identity, and thus the home becomes a positive space where we feel we belong and can flourish. I have also suggested that, for older lesbians and gay men in particular, the home is a place of vital importance. I have argued that for these reasons it is essential that care settings provide the opportunity for individuals to recreate these elements of home in any accommodation they provide. In the following section I will look more closely at the concerns that might arise for older lesbians and gay men who face entering supported accommodation.

Supported care settings

For the majority of older people the idea of entering supported accommodation is difficult and challenging, which may be partly due to the emotional distress associated with leaving their own home. This distress may be in the form of loss of 'personal identity, pain on leaving a place associated with valued memories, disruption of social networks and loss of the optimisation of daily functioning and coping engendered by a known familiar environment' (Dwyer, 2005, p.1081). The issue of supported accommodation is also widely discussed by older lesbians and gay men, with particular reference to whether or not there should be exclusively gay care homes and sheltered accommodation designed to meet the needs of this population and diminish some of the fears that are commonly raised. Studies (e.g. Heaphy et al., 2004a; Hubbard and Rossington, 1995; Places for People, 1999) have recently begun to discuss this question through exploring the housing needs of older lesbians and gay men. These studies have focused on what older people want – what would be their preference in terms of care – and thus far the overwhelming response has been that individuals want to end up receiving care that meets their individual needs as a gay person.

Heaphy et al. (2004b) found that the 'majority viewed residential care and nursing homes as an "undesirable" or "highly undesirable" milieu for care' (p.892), with many lesbians and gay men fearing getting older and having to enter provision where their sexuality is not understood (Springfield, 2002). As Heaphy et al. (2004b) note, 'among non-heterosexuals, the usual anxiety that the option generates is heightened by the perceived threats to their identity and way of living' (p.892). This has resulted in the identification of two desirable types of accommodation: gay-specific care or gay-friendly care – both of which highlight the importance for gay people of the acknowledgement of sexuality in their care settings.

REFLECTION

The desire for gay-specific or gay-friendly care seems to stem from fear or anxiety about residential care. Please read the following quotes, taken from the Lifting the Lid *(2006) participants, and identify their main concerns about residential care. A discussion of the main points will follow.*

---

a) *There is still a need to talk and reminisce isn't there, and when everyone else is talking and reminiscing about their times with their husbands or their wives, what can we say?*

b) *As a lesbian I don't want to be isolated because I still want to maintain the identity that I've got...I don't want to be in a situation...where it is a heterosexual environment where I am going to be cared for, because that's going to negate a whole part of me.*

57

c) *Disregarding friendship and relationships when making choices for gay person and their care.*

d) *You've always got to watch what you say, so people that go into homes have to go into the closet and self-censoring themselves, you've got to...y'know the very tiring mode of censoring yourself, keeping the conversation neutral...no, I may be being pessimistic, but I think it is back to the closet.*

e) *Having known people in homes, it does rather give me the horrors, but the idea of having to face homophobia as well would compound any problems.*

f) *As you get older you like to talk of the past. In a heterosexual world this is a challenge and you find you constantly have to explain yourself.*

g) *The lack of all inclusive services and the concern that I might end up in a home where my sexuality is a problem and is not understood.*

h) *Being constrained regarding expressing myself if I lived in such as residential or sheltered accommodation.*

i) *I think it would be very isolating. It is bad enough going into a home these days where people are lumped together regardless of whether they have anything in common anyway, but what a lot of men and women do have in common is their heterosexual lives and their children...I do think it is important to have some other people who shared some of my experiences.*

Discussion

These quotes give just a taster of the concerns older lesbians and gay men have about entering residential care in particular, but also moving into any accommodation which takes away their control over their environment. I have categorised these concerns as homophobia, heterosexism, loss of identity and ignorance of need.

Homophobia (quote e)
This relates to a fear of homophobia and discrimination from staff or other residents, particularly at a time when you are already vulnerable. Homophobia is documented well elsewhere in this book, so I will not dwell on it here, other than to highlight that, at the stage of entering residential care, to a large extent individuals are at the mercy of other people and are unable to walk away. Although you would hope that you wouldn't be subject to homophobia from staff, it does happen, and older gay people can be vulnerable to abuse. This may particularly be the case for isolated older people, who perhaps do not have the support of a partner, friends or family – someone on the outside who is looking out for them. A related fear is how other residents will treat gay people and, if homophobia does arise, how this will be dealt with by the home.

Heterosexism (Quotes a, b, f, i)
This relates to the fear of being placed in a heterosexual environment and just not fitting in, which is possibly the most consistently highlighted concern for older lesbians and gay

men, as residential care conjures up the image of being in a totally heterosexual setting, feeling cut off from any sense of a gay community, and instead spending days with people with whom you have little or nothing in common, leading to a fear of isolation.

While there may not be out-and-out homophobia to contend with, individuals are more likely to be subject to heterosexism, defined as 'the ideological system that denies, denigrates and stigmatises any non heterosexual form of behaviour, identity, relationship, or community' (Herek, 1995, in Langley, 2001, p.920). This could include, for example, assuming everyone is heterosexual until they tell you otherwise (e.g. 74 per cent of respondents in Neville and Henrickson [2006] said their healthcare provider assumed they were heterosexual), or an 'over emphasis on including families, e.g. grandchildren, in care-home activities' which 'may result in the exclusion or discouragement of prospective lesbian, gay and transsexual residents' (Springfield, 2002, p.586).

Heterosexism may well be evident in the residential home, as often 'mainstream and local communities tend to encourage and enforce a "heterosexual panorama" through legal, social and everyday sanctions against public displays of homosexuality' (Heaphy et al., 2004b, p.892). So, although there is generally an increased tolerance of homosexuality, there is still a risk of being 'out' which could lead to exclusion and feelings of being ostracised. Heaphy et al. (2004b) suggests that risking being out could potentially 'compromise their sense of belonging to local communities and put considerable pressure on them to remain closeted in all manner of community interactions' (p.892).

A loss of sexual identity (quotes d, h)
McAuliffe et al. (2007) define sexuality as:

> *A broad concept that encompasses the act of sex, as well as the expression of one's sexual identity, orientation, needs, function and preferences through thoughts, feelings and behaviour. It incorporates intimacy, romance, sensuality, eroticism and relationships, and is an important contributing factor to an individual's quality of life and well-being (p.69).*

Given the scope of sexuality, it seems to be important for individuals to feel at ease in being able to express it, as to hide something that has such an effect on their quality of life and well-being is surely detrimental. However, unless the individual chooses to disclose his/her sexuality, the assumption is likely to be one of heterosexuality; and 'if residents are presumed to be heterosexual, then there is no recognition that lesbian and gay people have differing needs' (Springfield, 2002, p.586). Brown (1998) also suggests that sexual identity is largely invisible to social workers.

Ignorance of need (Quotes c, g)
This referred particularly to issues such as the acknowledgement of partners and social support networks. In order to have a holistic understanding of an older gay person and their needs, it is essential that some consideration is given to the alternative social support networks which may be in place in an individual's life. A care assessment which ignores this aspect is likely to be counterproductive, potentially cutting off vital support, which could leave the individual more isolated and in much greater need of services. For example, suggesting a day centre could have the effect of increasing isolation 'if an older

lesbian or gay man cannot talk about their life for fear of discrimination, or where their experiences and things that matter to them are totally different from those of the other people who attend' (Langley, 2001, p.929). An appropriate care package would therefore be one which encompasses, and even encourages, the ongoing maintenance of the individual's social support network.

It is widely accepted that social support is important for older people and, for older lesbians and gay men, this support is more often derived from friends or partners than biological families (Herdt et al., 1997; Langley, 2001). This is most likely because of the withdrawal of family support as a result of the person's sexuality (Francher and Henkin, 1973, cited in Pugh, 2005). Familial support is often therefore 'replaced by friendship networks which become key in understanding how older lesbians and gay men live their lives and express their culture' (Pugh, 2005, p.212). This reliance on friendship has been borne out in several research projects, such as Heaphy et al. (2004a), who found that many participants described their friends as being the most important people in their lives, while half the participants agreed that their friends were their family. He also highlighted that, for emotional support, 58.6 per cent first turned to friends, with only 9 per cent turning to their families of origin.

The support networks of older lesbians and gay men are often referred to as 'chosen families', which 'are likely to be made up of friends, partners, ex-partners and accepting family members of origin' (Heaphy et al 2004b, p.890). These can be understood as 'flexible, but often strong and supportive networks of friends, lovers and even family of origin which provide the framework for the development of mutual care, responsibility and commitment for many lesbians and gay men' (Weekes et al., 1999, cited in Heaphy et al., 2004b, p.890). One participant in 'Lifting the Lid' (Gay and Grey, 2006) highlighted the potential benefit as 'living within a chosen family means that we are together out of choice and so stick together for reasons other than biological family duty. I am convinced that I am less likely to be lonely or abandoned as I grow older, than the heterosexual who relies on the biological family' (p.34).

Although the support of the chosen family and the gay community is not every gay person's experience, and indeed some are undoubtedly very isolated throughout their lives and in old age, those who are lucky enough to have support can benefit from its positive influence on physical and mental health. There is of course an acknowledgement that it can be difficult to maintain social contacts as you get older, but it is vital that older lesbians and gay men continue to have opportunities to meet and socialise, which should be taken into account in care assessments.

One further need which is often ignored in supported accommodation is sexual need. Bauer et al. (2007) suggest that 'the assumptions that older people are asexual and without sexual desires or feelings remain widespread, and the subject of older people and sex is still largely taboo' (p.64). Given this, along with older lesbians and gay men remaining invisible, it is more than likely that their sexual needs will not even be contemplated in a care assessment. Little research has been conducted on the sexual needs of older lesbians and gay men. However, 'Lifting the Lid' (Gay and Grey, 2006) found that 75.8 per cent of participants had sexual needs and 58.2 per cent said an active sex life was important to them. When discussing her concerns about residential care, one participant wanted to ensure that 'none of my identity, none of who I am, is amputated and that includes my sexuality and my sexual needs – from playful flirting, to making love with women' (p.37), highlighting the importance that both sex and sexuality continue to have in old age.

Based on this it would seem important that assessments should take sexual needs into account. This may include provision for partners to have privacy, or ensuring single people continue, as mentioned above, to have opportunities to meet and socialise with other gay people, whether that be for companionship or in order to seek opportunities to fulfil their own sexual needs. This is, however, an area which would benefit from further research.

Disclosure

Following from the above discussion regarding the concerns older gay people have about care settings, I will consider one issue in more detail, that of disclosure of sexuality. Various questions arise around this topic, such as whose responsibility is it, what factors might influence an individual to disclose, and is there any need for them to disclose anyway? So, in this section I will look at disclosure from the viewpoint of both the individual and the professional.

Individuals
At the heart of this issue is the personal choice of the older lesbian or gay man to either disclose their sexuality or to keep it hidden, and these options, along with some of the factors informing this decision, are considered below.

Back to the closet – hiding one's sexuality
To avoid potential homophobia or heterosexism, older lesbians and gay men may choose to 'pass' as heterosexual. 'Passing' is a term which describes the behaviour of lesbians and gay men to avoid being identified as gay, which highlights how gay people may differ from other oppressed groups in that they can hide their difference (Langley, 2001). Klitzman and Greenberg (2002, in Neville and Henrickson, 2006) found that many gay people see disclosing their sexuality as a risk. They found that this fear frequently results in either hiding sexual orientation or refusing to access services, and that both a fear of homophobic reactions and previous negative experiences are the main influences on whether a gay person will choose to disclose their sexuality to a professional. The risks with this strategy could include lack of consultation with their partner regarding care, lack of acknowledgement, no understanding of need, isolation, invisibility, having to constantly watch what they say – the list is extensive.

A leap in the dark – disclosing sexuality
The potential risks with disclosure include homophobia, mistreatment and judgement. The potential benefits, however, seem to outweigh this, possibly affording care which meets their needs and is appropriate to their lifestyle, acknowledgement of significant others, feeling validated, and in short, one less thing to worry about given that this is likely to be at a time of crisis when there are lots of other major concerns.

It is perhaps worth pointing out that this decision around disclosure is one that every gay person has to consider on a regular basis. This is not a 'unique event: they must choose whether or not to self disclose in every new situation and environment' (Neville and Henrickson, 2006, p.409). This is a very individual experience and, as a professional, it is worth bearing in mind that some people will have been coming out regularly since their teens, while some will only have realised their sexuality in their 50s and 60s and so may be still coming to terms with it. Some will have experienced prejudice and so be anxious about disclosing, others will disclose without even thinking about it. However, what gay people have in common is the need to constantly assess whether it is necessary to come out and whether it's safe to come out, and as Brown (1998) comments, this can be an exhausting process.

Professionals

Is it any of our business?

One of the biggest challenges for professionals working with this population is that they may not know which of their service users are lesbian or gay – and if they don't know, how can they work effectively with these service users? Social workers are already likely to be working with this group, but 'it does not follow that they will know who they are, as this is a group often characterised by its invisibility' (Langley, 2001, p.917). Coupled with this is the argument, as suggested above, that older gay people have a right to choose whether or not to disclose their sexual orientation to professionals.

In addition to this, some professionals have raised the argument that it is none of their business if a service user is gay, suggesting that sexuality is a personal issue which doesn't need to be known. This is often followed by the premise that 'we treat everyone the same'. Needless to say we are not all the same and to be treated as such would be oppressive. On this basis, assessments should be holistic and take account of all the individual's needs. Moreover, Harrison (2001, cited in Hughes, 2003, p.260) suggests that 'this privacy argument can be seen as a potentially dangerous copout and a serious obstacle to people realising their human potential with their sexual identities as integral'.

So what we potentially have here is a situation whereby professionals may not know if a service user they are working with is gay; the individual involved is perfectly within their rights not to disclose their sexuality, and professionals may not feel that they want to know anyway. It is this situation, however, that may have contributed to the ongoing invisibility of older lesbian and gay service users. This invisibility is perpetuated by policies which continue to exclude older gay people; for example, the National Service Framework (DoH, 2001) 'highlights particular minority groups within the older population, but fails to mention lesbians and gay men...with the resultant probability that they are invisible in practice' (Pugh, 2005, p.216). This invisibility suggests that the specific care needs of older lesbians and gay men are not necessarily being acknowledged, which Pugh (2005) sees as being reflected in 'the practice of health and social care professionals who may, as a result, be in breech of their legislative duty' (p.207). To combat this, Hughes (2003) highlights the need for 'talking about sexual identity in order to prevent it being rendered invisible' (p.258).

Neville and Henrickson (2006) also point out that 'knowing a person's sexual identity is pivotal in being able to gain access, understand, accurately assess and provide a high quality health service to this frequently marginalised group' (p.408). After all, as Bayliss (2000) suggests, 'an assessment based on partial information can itself only be partial' (p.48).

How can professionals talk to individuals about their sexuality?

I think it is important here to recognise that sexuality is not an easy issue to discuss, for either the professional or the older person. However, as professionals, we have a responsibility to at least get past the initial discomfort, if it is in the best interests of the service user. We should also acknowledge that the onus shouldn't necessarily be on the older person to make the first move regarding disclosure because 'the individual who is having needs assessed may require assistance and this may be at a time when that person is unwell. To expect that person to engage in the "exhausting" process of coming out at this time and having to manage the reaction is to expect a great deal' (Pugh, 2005, p.215).

What professionals can do to ease the process is to ensure from the outset that the language used, and the questions asked, are inclusive. The use of open questions should give individuals the freedom to respond, giving as much information as they feel comfortable with and should 'allow people to describe significant relationships without the need for denial or deceit' (Langley, 2001, p.928). As with guidelines for all assessments professionals undertake, questions should avoid judgements and, in this case particularly, assumptions. The slightest detail, such as asking about a partner rather than whether they are married, alerts the individual to the fact that you consider there are possibilities other than heterosexuality, and nuances such as this can really increase an individual's confidence in you. Higgins et al. (2006) further suggest that professionals should 'avoid language with a heterosexual bias', remarking that 'assumptions about whether or not the patient is sexually active, age and marital status are not determinants of whether a person is engaging in sexual intercourse or other intimate acts' (p.346).

As a final point in this section I would highlight that there may be a need to offer additional assurances of confidentiality to ensure older gay people have confidence to disclose their sexuality, and no assumption should be made that, because they have told you, they have told other people (Springfield, 2002). It may be obvious, perhaps, but you should always check with the individual concerned before discussing their sexuality with other professionals, family members, or indeed other residents.

REFLECTION

A gay service user about to go into residential care or sheltered accomodation may have some or all of the questions displayed below.

Take some time now to think about how you might resond to such questions. How confident are you that their needs would be met in the residential care homes you are aware of? How confident would you feel about approaching the care home and discussing these issues with them on be half of the service user?

- *Who can I talk to about my needs?*
- *Will my sexuality be acknowledged?*
- *Will staff be aware of my needs?*
- *Will my partner be kept informed of my care needs?*
- *Will I be discriminated against by staff?*
- *Will my support network be acknowledged?*
- *Will I have anything in common with other residents?*

- *Will my gay friends be welcome to visit?*
- *Will I be able to share a room with my partner?*
- *Will I become invisible?*
- *Will I be discriminated against by other residents?*
- *How will I get privacy with my partner?*

Summary

In this section it has been argued that older gay people have particular concerns regarding entering supported accommodation, which relate to their sexuality. The four main concerns are around homophobia, heterosexism, loss of identity and ignorance of need. Given these issues and the suggestion that their needs will not be met, some older lesbians and gay men have voiced the need for services to be provided specifically for them. One study found that 80 per cent of participants felt there should be lesbian- and gay-specific accommodation (Places for People, 1999), while 'Lifting the Lid' (Gay and Grey, 2006) found that over three-quarters of participants wanted their sexuality to be taken into account. However, the overwhelming theme in both these pieces of research is that older gay people want care that is individualised and that understands and acknowledges sexuality as an important part of identity.

Home-care

As discussed above, the majority of older people would rather retain their independence and stay in their own home as long as possible. It has also been explored why the home could be of particular importance for older gay people. There are, however, some issues which need to be taken into consideration for home-care, many of which reflect those discussed above.

- **Incoming carers will need to be aware that individuals may or may not feel comfortable enough to disclose their sexuality.**

Gorman-Murray (2006) describes examples from research (e.g. Kirby and Hay, 1997) which suggest that some gay couples continue to choose to maintain a heterosexual 'front', such as having unused separate bedrooms, 'in order to convince straight visitors there is no intimate relationship', or who modify the home environment when visitors are expected: ' sexuality-identifying objects are concealed when straight neighbours, family members or trades people visit'. This is obviously far from ideal and could hinder 'the performance of gay/lesbian identities in these domestic environments' (p.148). The carer must therefore be aware that some individuals will go to great lengths to conceal their sexuality and, as already discussed, the carer should do all they can to take the onus off the individual to disclose, while giving gentle support and encouragement – providing a safe environment in which the individual would feel safe to come out should they wish to do so.

If you consider again someone like Harold who has protected their identity and environment fiercely through the home setting, it is understandable that having an unknown carer may present a threat to this safe world that he has so carefully constructed. Anecdotal evidence suggests that many gay people, even those who are very comfortable with their sexuality, may feel a discomfort about strangers entering their homes. For example, with visiting tradespeople, the thought will inevitably arise – will they be OK with me being gay? Strangers induce vulnerability, particularly when they enter into your sanctuary, and particularly at a time when you are vulnerable.

- **Carers will need to take into account the individual's social support network, to explore who the important people are in their lives – partners, friends, family, etc.**

Once again this comes down to avoiding assumptions, either that the individual is isolated because they have no family, or that they are part of a supportive network of gay people. What came across from participants in 'Lifting the Lid' (Gay and Grey, 2006) was that the most important characteristics for a carer were a) that they were good carers, and b) that they were gay-friendly.

The following quotes highlight this:

Gay-friendly personal care is the only acceptable form (p.29).

She must know that I am a lesbian and accept that, otherwise I would want a lesbian carer (p.29).

My main concern would be that my carer would understand and respect my sexuality (p.29).

Well very nice to stay in your own home…but then you really do want some gay nurse or gay-friendly nurse to come round. You wouldn't want one that's not friendly…because when a care helper comes in…you want a nice attitude and give you a nice day (p.63).

Chapter summary

This chapter has attempted to highlight and discuss some of the prevalent issues regarding older lesbians and gay men and care settings. It is argued that older lesbians and gay men may have specific issues and concerns, as distinct from the older population in general. The home has been presented here as important, both as a personal space and a social space, and it is recommended that these aspects should be replicated in care settings. The main concerns that older gay people have expressed with regards to entering supported accommodation are homophobia, heterosexism, loss of identity and ignorance of need. This chapter has argued for individualised assessments which highlight the needs of the whole person. It has also highlighted the need for the professional involved to take some responsibility for helping individuals disclose their sexuality. As a final point, it has highlighted that the overwhelming theme in most research concerning older gay people and supported care settings is the need for care which is individualised and that understands and acknowledges sexuality as an important part of identity.

Chapter 6

Looking forward: developing creativity in practice

By Christina Hicks

Previous chapters have looked at historical and contemporary experiences and influences on older lesbians and gay men, explored some of the developing body of research into their needs and proposed different ways of approaching practice. This chapter looks at their conclusions, the importance of social groups and networks, the impact of group acceptance and self-acceptance and suggests ways of enabling the development of creativity in practice with older lesbians and gay men.

Given that an estimated 10 per cent of the population identifies as lesbian or gay (Dulaney and Kelly, 1982, cited by Logan and Kershaw, 1994), it is highly likely that health and social care workers will encounter older lesbians and gay men. However, it is entirely probable that in the majority of cases they will not know. The key themes identified by the Gay and Grey research (2006) included the extent of the isolation that can be experienced; the need for gay-friendly services including advocacy, buddying and physical support; the importance of education and awareness training; codes of conduct that enshrine anti-discriminatory policies; and, perhaps most importantly, the desire for validation and acceptance.

In the foreword on the first page of the National Service Framework for Older People (Department of Health, 2004) the then Secretary of State, Alan Milburn, states 'Just like the rest of us, older people want to enjoy good health and remain independent for as long as possible. As people get older remaining independent often depends on health and social care services being effective enough to support them' (p.1). In order to be effective those services need to develop person-centred, holistic ways of working which take into account the cultural backgrounds of individuals.

In June 2006 the Department of Health published *Core Training Standards for Sexual Orientation: making Health Services inclusive for Lesbian, Gay and Bisexual (LGB) People*. This states that 'For LGB people the imperative for core training standards in sexual orientation is now reinforced by the Equalities Act 2006 which outlines regulations on the provision of goods and services…These regulations [will] make inclusion of LGB staff and service users/patients within health and social care a requirement' (Cree and O'Corra, 2006, p.5). So, in regulatory terms it is no longer acceptable to ignore the existence of lesbians and gay men and it requires practitioners to ensure they work in ways which not only meet the stipulations of the regulations but also the spirit.

As Pugh (2005) says, older lesbians and gay men do have cultural differences from other older people, and it is important that those differences are acknowledged in the ways in which services are provided. Assumptions cannot be made about what it is like to be an older lesbian or gay man; just as there are many ways of being an older person, there are many ways of being an older lesbian or gay man.

In highlighting the problems of isolation, lack of support and the need for social groups, the Gay and Grey report (2006) noted that those with good social contacts were more fulfilled, confirming findings in other studies such as Heaphy et al. (2003). It identified a lack of social venues and activities which were not 'alcohol focused', particularly for older gay men, although older lesbians seemed to have thriving and well-supported social groups. It is possible that the area covered by the research is particularly well served by such groups and this finding is therefore not illustrative of the country as a whole. Interestingly, the study carried out by Heaphy et al. (2004) identified a number of networks available to older gay men through which participants could be recruited; as fewer such networks were found for older lesbians, they concluded that women were more likely to rely on 'hidden' support. The apparent differences in the findings of these researchers again underline the diversity within a group frequently considered to be homogeneous.

However, evidence about the extent to which some may belong to social groups or networks does not mean that older lesbians do not suffer from the same feelings of isolation and fear as older gay men. Just as not all older people want to go to day centres or join social groups or clubs, not all older lesbians or gay men want to join existing groups. They may have a particular interest or skill that they would like to explore but don't have the organisational skills necessary to form a group. The mix of ages in most groups may be intimidating to some; younger lesbians and gay men have different experiences and may, like some other younger people, be impatient with the memories of those who are older. Many have little or no knowledge or understanding of how different things were for the older generations. Some lesbians of all ages, for example, are dismissive of older lesbians who were married and had children. They seem to see it as some sort of betrayal of their sexuality whereas it was more likely to have been a lack of choice or a means of survival.

Gay-Glos has developed Rural Friendship Groups in recognition of the problems than can be caused by lack of money, transport and friends, all of which can add to a sense of loneliness and isolation. They have also developed groups for those over the age of 60. As they say on their website, 'Friendship Support Groups give a sense of belonging, widen personal and social networks and support a stronger sense of well being' (www.gay-glos.org). While this website seemed to be inactive at the time it was accessed, the fact that it exists and that the work described therein was done illustrates that the need was there.

Although social groups as such will not meet the needs of everyone, it is important that ways of enabling people to maintain or develop social contacts are found. As has been highlighted in an earlier chapter, people feel they have control in their own homes and one possibility might be to find ways of enabling individuals to extend their social networks through 'at homes'. As with all human beings, one size does not fit all and it is essential that the individuality of people is identified and taken into consideration through working holistically. Sometimes the best and simplest solutions come from the individual themselves so it is important to listen to them and enable them to express what they want and how they consider they might achieve it.

The theories on the positive, negative and adverse effects of living with discrimination and of feeling the need to hide one's true nature are far too numerous and complex to cover in detail in this text. Briefly, though, one is the debate around the theory of cognitive dissonance, which occurs when we believe something about ourselves but act against it (Festinger, 1957, cited by David Straker, 2002). In this theory we feel we have to find a way of resolving the difference between our belief and our actions. We can do this by either ignoring it, changing one or the other or by finding a way of rationalising the dissonance. For example, a 'closeted' lesbian or gay man may decide the only way to rationalise the conflict is by assuming that they are wrong about themselves by denying their sexuality and acting as if they are heterosexual or asexual. It is not difficult to imagine what sort of long-term effect this may have on their general well-being or their mental health.

The social identity theory, developed by Tajfel and Turner in 1979 (cited in Holah and Davies [2006], proposes that the membership of social groups and categories forms an important part of our self-concept. Included in the underlying psychological mechanisms of this theory is that there is a tendency to use group membership as a source of self-esteem, and maintaining a positive self-esteem is a basic human motivation.

Few like to feel that they are 'out of the ordinary' and such feelings can militate against self-esteem and therefore, it could be argued, self-acceptance. Acceptance by a group could therefore enable and encourage positive self-esteem and self-acceptance. 'Living a lie' and not being a part of a group or society in which we can feel totally free to be ourselves can exacerbate feelings of loneliness and isolation as well as potentially cause damage to self-esteem and weaken self-acceptance. It must be recognised that an existing older lesbian or gay male social group may not be the most appropriate answer for an individual but it might be the source of information that will identify an acceptable way forward.

The separation from families and therefore from the support of the family has meant that older lesbians and gay men look to friendship to provide that support. In many ways this could have advantages over family-based support. Dorfman et al. (1995, cited in Pugh, 2005, p.212), state:

- friends are more likely to give freely and without obligations, whereas families have increased expectations and demands

- friends are more empathic listeners than families, who have vested interests in avoiding and denying difficult areas

- friends provide fun.

Additionally, friends are more likely to have had similar experiences and to have a greater understanding of concerns and problems encountered. Sadly, though, as we age so do our friends and we may find ourselves outliving many of them. As we get older it becomes more difficult to develop new friendships, especially if the opportunities to meet like-minded people are not there. This means that not only do our remaining friends become more precious but the likelihood of loneliness and isolation increases. As has been seen in previous chapters, the underlying concern about deciding whether or not to 'come out' becomes more exhausting with age and frailty. So, if safe ways of meeting older lesbians and gay men are not clearly available, staying hidden can be seen as being the 'easy' and most attractive option.

The depth and complexity of feelings around 'coming out' and the potential repercussions cannot be overemphasised. They can encompass fear, shame, guilt, embarrassment, insecurity, anger, frustration, resentment, rejection and more. Or it can be fairly straightforward, as in the case of a participant in the Gay and Grey (2006) research who said, *I do not like to have to make a public statement about an aspect of myself which is intensely personal* (p.20).

Given the continuing influence of the medical model on assessment (based on illness and debility) together with the limited nature of needs that can be met, it is not surprising that practice takes little account of the individuality of people. Also, there is the credence given to the denial of the sexuality of older people generally by failure in government advice (Department of Health, 1991) to acknowledge sexuality as an aspect of the lives of older people. So, alongside invisibility, ageism ensures that older lesbians and gay men are likely to experience a denial of sexuality, as this is what happens to all older people. In the unlikely event of any sexuality being assumed, that assumption will be one of heterosexuality. As has been shown in a previous chapter changes in legislation can take a long time to filter through to practice.

In her study of the views of academics in the helping professions in Israel, Adital Ben-Ari (2001) concluded that there is homophobia and proposes that it can be confronted in three ways: by self-awareness, by learning the facts and by personal encounters. She also concludes that the attitudes of social work students are less negative than those of their mentors. She highlights the strong demand that has been made for the inclusion of lesbian and gay issues in the curriculum of professional training and education in the helping professions but considers that there needs first to be a change in the attitudes of those responsible for that training and education. This is not likely to apply only to Israel, and the need for lesbian and gay issues to be specifically included in training is something that is highlighted in the Gay and Grey report (2006).

In their paper on heterosexism and social work education, Logan and Kershaw (1994) state that, 'In contrast to developments in relation to racism and sexism, little attention has been given to heterosexism – yet the heterosexual hegemony needs challenging with urgency if we are to truly work in an anti-oppressive way with lesbians and gay men' (p.61). They refer to the lack of emphasis on sexual orientation within CCETSW (Central Council for Education and Training in Social Work, superseded by the General Social Care Council in 2001) and point out the difference between the terms 'anti-discriminatory' and 'anti-oppressive'. That is, the former challenges unfairness whereas the latter works to 'a model of empowerment and liberation which requires a fundamental rethinking of values, institutions and relationships' (Logan and Kershaw, 1994, p.73). (The General Social Care

Council, 2002, issued Codes of Practice for Social Care Workers and Employers, which require a commitment to 'Respecting diversity and different cultures and values' – section 1.6.) Logan and Kershaw go on to state that the theoretical perspectives which direct social work are mostly taken from sociological and psychological theory which, when considering sexual orientation, are heavily influenced by deviancy theory. Added to this, most texts are heterosexist and/or ignore the existence of different sexualities. A big step forward could be taken if these influences were to be disregarded and replaced by the increasing amount of empirical evidence of the needs of lesbians and gay men of all ages that is now available.

Developing creativity

It is recognised that there will always be constraints on funding but a good deal can be done within those constraints and individuals can make a difference. By displaying sensitivity and empathy, the imaginative worker can find creative ways of developing their own work practices. There are many sources of information and examples of good practice that can be adapted or developed to have relevance to working with older lesbians and gay men. Not least of these are the individuals themselves, many of whom will have considerable understanding of their own needs and how they might be met.

Community development

In developing practice with older lesbians and gay men, much can be taken from the occupational standards of community development work, the key purpose of which is to:

collectively bring about social change and justice by working with communities to:

• *identify their needs, opportunities, rights and responsibilities*

• *plan, organise and take action*

• *evaluate the effectiveness and impact of the action;*

all in ways which challenge oppression and tackle inequalities (Federation for Community Development Learning).

This is not at odds with the assessment process or the General Social Care Council Codes of Practice for Social Care Workers; all that is necessary is to be open and receptive to the different experiences, beliefs and ways of life of others. Using their skills and knowledge in this way, social care workers can go a long way towards meeting the aspirations of older lesbians and gay men identified in '*Lifting the Lid on Sexuality and Ageing*' (Gay and Grey in Dorset, 2006).

Learning from others

It seems that services designed for older people are based on the premise that they are a distinct and homogeneous group which has little or no resemblance to, or connection with, other generations. It's as if they have materialised from a chrysalis and are unlike any other section of the population and therefore need to be treated differently. No thought is given to whether the lessons learned from working with other age groups can be utilised when working with older people. The issue is identified in *Out of the Shadows* (Manthorpe and Price, 2003) where the point is made that little thought has been given to translating good practice from work with young people and their families to older age groups. While that paper is specifically about people with dementia, the point is well made and is relevant to all services. Case studies from across the board, together with issues arising from complaints, could be useful tools in the continuing training, education and development of social care workers and services.

Direct payments

The Direct Payments Guidance (Department of Health, 2003) defines the purpose as 'to give recipients control over their own life by providing an alternative to social care services provided by a local council' (p.3). Being able to control who enters their home can be fundamental to an older lesbian or gay man making the decision to accept help, particularly if very personal care is needed. Imagine the difficulties inherent in receiving help with getting dressed or undressed, washing or using the toilet under any circumstances, then think of the additional anxieties created by the problem of 'coming out'. Also, given the sensitivities already discussed elsewhere, even with more impersonal services it can be crucial that the older lesbian or gay man is able to choose who should provide those services. The flexibility of receiving a financial payment enables this freedom and 'increases the opportunities for independence, social inclusion and enhanced self-esteem' (Department of Health, 2003, p.3). An additional consideration in the context of direct payments is the government expectation that a greater number of older people should receive them.

Age Concern guidance

Age Concern (2001), as part of its Opening Doors project, developed a good practice guidance resource pack. This contains many ideas of how to work with older lesbians and gay men and make services more welcoming and friendly. It covers the differences between older lesbians and gay men and points out that 'older lesbians count amongst the poorest groups in society despite greater participation in the workforce than older heterosexual women' (p.16). It also gives a list of ten services that 'need to be welcoming and appropriate to all' (p.17), although this list is not exclusive. They include income and pensions advice, housing needs, transport information, practical help in and around the home, arts and culture, etc.

Additionally, it gives a list of ten myths and misinterpretations such as 'There aren't any around here', 'We're open to everyone anyway' and 'No-one's ever asked so there's obviously no need' (Age Concern, 2001, pp.17–22) There is also practical advice on getting started which encompasses such things as inviting lesbian and gay speakers to meetings, offering meeting space to lesbian and gay groups, inviting lesbian and gay groups to appropriate events, and not using openly or obviously homophobic service providers. It goes on to cover what individuals can do and gives ideas for services. Although it was published in 2001 before the Civil Partnership Act 2004 and the Equality Act (Sexual Orientation) Regulations 2007, it contains much good advice. It is a fairly comprehensive resource and is available as a PDF through the Age Concern website (www.ageconcern.org.uk/ openingdoors).

Advocacy

A Community Care special report *Advocacy and Older People* (Hocking, 2006) concluded that the benefits of advocacy for excluded and vulnerable older people are clear and now need to be promoted widely to social care staff and service users. The report highlighted the lack of availability of advocacy for older people and the lack of knowledge and awareness of both social workers and service users. The need for and lack of advocacy services is also highlighted in the Gay and Grey report (2006, p.64), where one respondent said:

> *The other area where I feel I need help is advocacy, sometimes, not just the care aspect, it's how I handle my money. Stuff like that. And who can you trust? So an advocacy service of some type, one that you could trust...*

Previous chapters in this text have covered the problems related to 'coming out' and the increasing difficulties faced by people as they become frail and more vulnerable. Like all older people, lesbians and gay men do not want to have to keep on battling for recognition of their needs and are inclined to withdraw and do without. Given the necessity to be completely open and candid with an advocate, it is even more important that older lesbians and gay men in need of such services have confidence that there is someone who truly understands and can convey their needs. Without that, even if advocacy services are available, they are likely to refuse to use one, thereby disadvantaging themselves further.

Bereavement

The need for lesbian and gay-focused bereavement services was highlighted by the Gay and Grey research (2006). As one participant in the research said:

> *After he died...I went into a sort of deep, deep depression...I had bereavement counselling through my GP* [not gay-specific] *it was helpful I suppose...the hardest thing I think...was people didn't realise...that bereavement in a gay relationship could be so brutal...'* (p.64)

When talking about a bereavement evening, another respondent said

> *They sub-divide you into smaller groups...you just get to tell your story...there's no guarantee that people are going to be accepting...it puts homosexuality on the table, when actually all that I care about is the fact that my partner's died and I'm hurting...I would have preferred to have been with other gay people...I would have liked there to have been some kind of acknowledgement of my relationship with [her]...I think more than anything else there is a need for gay bereavement counselling.* (p.65)

Bereavement is a particularly vulnerable time for everybody and it would appear that little has been done to identify or provide for older lesbians and gay men who lose partners or close friends. Whereas the loss of a loved one usually elicits great sympathy, this is not always the case where the loss is of a same-sex partner. All the previously discussed issues around 'coming out' apply with the added distress of coping with grief and a general lack of understanding and support. It is difficult enough to deal with the emotions of bereavement and loss of intimacy and companionship, and the emptiness and loneliness that follow death, without having to consider anything else.

This also brings to the fore the question of services provided by funeral directors and the availability of lesbian- and gay-friendly funeral ceremonies. There may be some, but they might not be easy to find or be in the immediate locality, and if you are unable to be open how do you locate them? A worker who endeavoured to ensure that lesbian- and gay-friendly bereavement and funeral services were either readily available or easily identified would be providing a considerable service. This might be achieved by working with existing services to enable them to be inclusive and aware of the needs of differing sexualities as well as those of differing cultures and faiths.

Buddying

A 'buddy' is someone who is separate from the services who you can talk to about how you are feeling or what problems you may have. They can also help with accessing both voluntary and other services and finding out about possible interest or support groups. It is someone who is of a similar age and, ideally, has had similar experiences and can provide company when going out, perhaps to a support group. In the main it seems that the buddying schemes that are available are for schoolchildren and those with learning disabilities or mental health problems. However, buddies could be a very positive resource for older lesbians and gay men, potentially enabling them to develop the confidence to interact with the local community, both gay and heterosexual.

User participation

In many areas there will be older lesbians and gay men who are willing to interact with professionals and provide information and advice on making services gay-friendly. They may also be prepared to participate in training programmes or attend/speak at local meetings, conferences or seminars. They can be a valuable resource and one that is little, if ever, used. Citizens Advice Bureau, Age Concern, Tourist Information, Yellow Pages and Directory Enquiries are all places where information about local lesbian or gay male social groups may be found.

Reminiscence

Older lesbians and gay men are no different from the many older people who enjoy looking back and sharing with others their memories of bygone days. Historically, knowledge and experience were passed on through the telling of stories and today children can learn much about their family and cultural history through listening to the tales of their grandparents and other older relatives. It enables the older person to relive some of their experiences, can promote consideration and acceptance, and can give a sense of continuity and of the past.

The value of reminiscence is increasingly being recognised in working with older people and those with dementia. Just as in individual families, cross and intergenerational work can help in breaking down barriers and developing understanding. Both can be seen in the work done by Age Exchange in their Intergenerational Arts and Learning programme, which uses reminiscence as its source (www.age-exchange.org.uk). If managed with sensitivity and care, reminiscence could help to reduce feelings of loneliness and isolation and possibly encourage greater involvement in and with the local community.

Mental health

The particular needs of those with mental health problems are not within the scope of this publication. Nevertheless, some comment needs to be made in view of the potential for mental health problems to develop if sexuality is dismissed or ignored. In *Women's Mental Health: Into the Mainstream*, the Department of Health (2002) puts forward its plans for developing mental health care for women. It recognises that social factors have an influence on mental health and refers explicitly to the vulnerability of lesbian and bisexual women. It is important to be aware of the fact that many older lesbians and gay men have in the past been treated as if they had a mental health problem. Clearly, those experiences will to a greater or lesser extent influence their response to health and social care workers.

In 2003 the Social Perspectives Network (SPN) published a presentation, 'Lesbian and gay perspectives on mental distress' given by a lesbian who experiences mental health problems. In this address, the speaker, Sarah Carr, gives a very clear summation of her experiences which include her early inappropriate encounters with therapists. They include a diagnostic method which involved being shown male-oriented 'top shelf' pornography. As she did not find them sexually appealing, the conclusion was that she couldn't be gay. The assumption, presumably, was that if she was a lesbian she would have been aroused in the same way as a man might be. This demonstrates a complete lack of understanding of what being a lesbian means. After describing the difficulties she had encountered and eventually overcome she concludes that:

> The normalising experience of being with people who accept me for who I am has been very significant. I have, like many other gay people, formed my own 'chosen family' because my biological family is too often the site of denial, conflict and distress. (Carr, 2003, p.36)

She goes on the say how beneficial it was to find a lesbian therapist because it 'has meant that I have been able to positively benefit from therapeutic treatment, because my sexuality is not a problem for or to her' (p.36).

Summary

To summarise, the ways in which you could consider developing creativity in your practice might include:

- thinking about how the key purpose of community development work might be helpful

- looking at what other sectors of the services (particularly those for children and young people) are doing/have done and see if their ideas can be developed in working with older lesbians and gay men

- considering how direct payments might be of benefit in enabling an individual to exercise choice over who should provide care, especially personal and intimate care

- considering the Age Concern Resource Pack and the Core Training Standards for Sexual Orientation (Cree and O'Corra, 2006) developed by the Department of Health and Sexual Orientation and Gender Identity Equality Advisory Group

- finding out what advocacy, bereavement and buddying services exist and considering how they might be used as a template or developed to encompass the needs of older lesbians and gay men

- exploring how reminiscence groups might be set up, possibly including cross-generational working, mixing both heterosexual and lesbian and gay people

- engaging with voluntary organisations, including those for lesbians and gay men, and looking at what they are doing/have to offer

- actively promoting a policy of inviting older lesbians and gay men to meetings and more informal networking events and as speakers

- finding ways of engaging with training departments to influence the development of appropriate training programmes and the potential use of older lesbians and gay men in those programmes

- using this text to explore your own prejudices and misconceptions and develop ways of being truly accepting.

Glossary

Ageism	Assumptions and prejudice made on grounds of age
Bisexual	Sexually attracted to people of both sexes
Coming out	Declaring one's homosexuality to self, friends or the world at large
Continuous disclosure	Having to declare one's sexuality continuously throughout life
Gay	General name for homosexual men – now gradually becoming a favoured term to embrace homosexual women (by some lesbians)
Gay scene	Specific lesbian and gay culture involving commercially run pubs and clubs
GLF	Gay Liberation Front
Heterosexism	Discrimination or prejudice by heterosexuals against or towards homosexuals
Homophobia	A dislike, a fear or a prejudice against homosexuals
Internalised homophobia	An unconscious assimilation of established homophobia
LAGLO	Lesbian and Gay Liaison Officers
Lesbian	Homosexual woman
Lesbian- and gay-friendly	Total acceptance of lesbian and gay men's sexuality, lifestyles and culture
LGBT	Lesbian, gay, bisexual and transsexual
Marginalise	Treat as insignificant and exclude from mainstream of society
MCC	Metropolitan Community Church
PAR	Participatory action research
Participatory action research	A research methodology which is undertaken 'with' people rather than 'on' people
Sampling	Taking a selection of individuals from distinct groups of the population for investigation
Snowball sampling	A convenient way of collecting samples by word of mouth – person to person
Transgender	The physical characteristics of one sex and the supposed psychological characteristics of another

Timeline on homosexuality and the law

By Ann Fannin

630–00 BC: Greece and the Roman Empire. It is difficult to get a clear picture of how same-sex love was regarded in the years BC. However, there are clues. In ancient Greece there were several references to male homosexuality (there was no word for same-sex love in that era – that came much later, in the nineteenth century; however, for my purposes at this time I will refer to same-sex relationships as either homosexual, lesbian or gay). There were many writings dealing with homoerotic love in myths, tales of ancient gods, plays and written discourses. In Plato's time (427–347 BC) same-sex love between men was not only regarded as the highest form of love, but it was taken for granted that men were attracted to beauty in both young men and women. Apart from Sappho, the well-known lesbian poet of ancient Greece in 630 BC, little is known of lesbian love, but the fact that Sappho, was never censored for her lesbian poems or for her open love of women would suggest that same-sex love between women was regarded as acceptable and normal.

...no one in the early Roman world seemed to feel that the fact that someone preferred his or her own gender was any more significant than the fact that someone preferred blue eyes or short people. (John Boswell, 1979)

According to Boswell, gay marriage, for both males and females, was legal and frequent. In Thebes, a regiment of 500 soldiers, made up entirely of gay men, was regarded as the epitome of courage and valour. There appear to be no references to gay life in Britain BC.

AD 1200–1533: In Britain in particular, there seems to have been a wealth of popular gay art and literature around in the eleventh and twelth centuries, and there was a revival of gay culture, particularly among clerics and monks (Boswell, 1979). Later on in the thirteenth century, attitudes changed. In 1290 there was the first formal record of this growing tension towards homosexual men. An anonymous jurist at the court of James I declared that sodomites should be buried alive. For the next several centuries, sodomy (for both heterosexual and homosexual relationships) was seen as unnatural and deemed a vice. There were several different harsh punishments declared, from being burnt alive to being hanged.

1533: The Buggery Act. Passed in 1533 (punishable by hanging), this Act was repealed and re-enacted several times during the reigns of Henry VIII, Edward VI and Queen Mary. Finally,

Queen Elizabeth I re-enacted it in 1563, which laid the basis for the criminalisation of the act of sodomy for the next several centuries. The 1700s onwards saw prejudice towards homosexuality becoming rife in the general public, with the Church issuing several anti-gay pamphlets and assorted literature. It had now become 'A crime not to be named by Christians' (William Blackstone's commentaries, 1765–69, quoted in Boswell, 1979).

1861: The Offences Against the Person Act abolished the death penalty for buggery.

1885: Criminal Law Amendment Act. Until the passing of this Act, any law pertaining to sexual activity had been limited to sodomy or buggery of either sex. In this Act, Henry Labouchére focused specifically on outlawing sex between two (or more) men. This Act effectively made male homosexuality illegal and generally became known as 'the blackmailer's charter'.

1956: The Sexual Offences Act saw little change in law as far as male sexual relationships were concerned and was merely a consolidation of the existing provisions. This Act was to precipitate a lot of police activity against homosexuals for many years.

1957: The Wolfenden Report was published. This report, headed by Sir John Wolfenden, concluded that 'homosexuality should no longer be a crime' (http://news.bbc.co.uk/onthisday) stating that what people do in the privacy of their own homes was 'not the law's business' (ibid). The Archbishop of Canterbury at the time supported the proposals in the report, but Parliament rejected the recommendation.

1967: The Sexual Offences Act: In the early years of the 1960s there was a steady increase in campaigning against the criminalisation of homosexuals, culminating in the decriminalisation (in England and Wales only) of private homosexual acts between two men aged over 21.

1988: Section 28 of the Local Government Act stated that 'A local authority shall not a) intentionally promote homosexuality or publish material with the intention of promoting homosexuality; b) promote the teaching in any maintained school of the acceptability of homosexuality as a pretend family relationship' (Office of Public Sector Information).

1994: The age of consent for sex between two men was lowered from 21 to 18 years.

1997: Government recognised (in certain circumstances) same-sex relationships for immigration purposes.

1997: A ruling from the Law Lords was passed, entitling same-sex partners equal tenancy rights as heterosexuals.

2000: The ban on homosexuals serving in the army was lifted by the British government.

2001: The Sexual Offences (Amendment) Act reduced the minimum age of consent from 18 to 16 years and this Act also declared male rape a criminal offence.

2003: Section 28 of the Local Government Act was repealed.

2003: Employment Equality (Sexual Orientation) Regulations. These regulations made it illegal to discriminate in any way against lesbians, gay men or bisexuals in the workplace (Statutory Instrument 2003 No.1661).

2005: Section 146 of the Criminal Justice Act 2003 was implemented. This section commissioned the courts to 'increase sentences for aggravation related to disability or sexual orientation' (Office of Public Sector Information).

2005: The Civil Partnership Act came into effect on 5 December 2005. Although not called marriage (religious organisations have yet to agree to weddings in places of worship), a civil ceremony now gives same-sex partnerships the same legal status as heterosexual marriage.

2005: The Adoption and Children's Act 2002 (Consequential Amendments) Order 2005 was implemented on 30 December, giving rights to same-sex couples who wanted to adopt children.

2007: The Equality Act (Sexual Orientation). The 'goods and services' Act which effectively makes it illegal to discriminate against people on grounds of sexual orientation in any way (Statutory Instrument 2007 No 1263).

References and background reading

BBC News (2007) *On This Day* 4 September (http://news.bbc.co.uk/onthisday) (accessed 26 September 2007).

Boswell John (1979) *The Church and the Homosexual: An Historical Perspective*. www.fordham.edu/halsall/pwh/1979boswell.html (accessed 26 September 2007).

Civil Partnership Act 2004. Office of Public Sector Information www.opsi.gov.uk/acts/acts2004/20040033.htm (accessed 26 September 2007).

Equality Act (Sexual Orientation) Regulations 2007 www.opsi.gov.uk/si/si2007/20071263.htm (accessed 26 September 2007).

Employment Equality (Sexual Orientation) Regulations 2003: Statutory Instrument 2003 No. 1661. www.opsi.gov.uk/SI/si2003/20031661.htm (accessed 26 September 2007).

Criminal Justice Act 2003 Section 146. HMSO www.legislation.gov.uk/acts/acts2003/ukpga (accessed 26 September 2007).

Stanford Encyclopaedia of Philosophy. Homosexuality. http://plato.stanford.edu/entries/homosexuality (accessed 26 September 2007).

Stonewall 'Sexual Offences' www.stonewall.org.uk/information_bank/criminal_law/69.asp (accessed 26 September 2007).

The Greater London Authority's Sexual Orientation Equality Scheme: From Isolation to Inclusion December 2006.

The Knitting Circle *Timetable of lesbian and gay history*. www.knittingcircle.org.uk/timetable.html (accessed 26 September 2007).

Weeks, J. (1989) *Sex, Politics and Society: The regulation of sexuality since 1800*. London: Longman.

Wilson, C. (2007) LGBT politics and sexual liberation. *International Socialism*, 114, Spring.

Useful contacts and resources

London Lesbian and Gay Switchboard (24 hours)
(A mine of information on all lesbian, gay and bisexual issues)
Telephone 020 7837 73324
www.llgs.org.uk

Stonewall
(British campaigning group for LGBT equality and justice)
Tower Building
York Road
London
SE1 7NX
Telephone 020 7593 1877
Email info@stonewall.org.uk

Age Concern LGBT
National Development and policy officer for older lesbians, gay men and bisexuals
Telephone 020 8765 7576
Age Concern (general)
Astra House
1268 London Road
London SW16 4ER
Free Helpline 0800 009966

GALOP anti-violence and policing
(This is primarily for the London area, but they will help for other calls)
PO Box 32810
London N1 3ZD
Telephone 020 7704 6767
Email info@galop.org.uk

Crimestoppers
(To report homophobic hate crime)
Telephone 0800 555 111

Independent Police Commission
(Handles complaints against the police)
Telephone 08453 002 002

National Friend
(social contact, information and helplines throughout the country for lesbians and gay men)
The Custard Factory
216 Gibb Street
Birmingham B9 4AA
Tel 0121 684 1261

Polari
(working for better services for older LGBT people)
5th Floor
Central House
14 Upper Woburn Place
London WC1H 0AE
Telephone 020 7255 4480
Email info-polari@madasafish.com

Kenrick: National Lesbian Social Organisation
Telephone 0870 765 8850
Email kenricINFO@aol.com

Alzheimer's Society Lesbian and Gay Network
Telephone Helpline 0845 300 0336
Email **gay carers@alzheimers.org.uk**
www.alzheimers.org.uk

Terrence Higgins Trust
(AIDS advice)
52–54 Gray's Inn Road
London WC1X
Telephone 020 7831 0330

Black Lesbian and Gay Helpline
Telephone 020 7837 5364 (Thursdays 7–10pm)

Imaan
(LGB Muslim people)
PO Box 5369
London W1A 6SD
Telephone 07849 170793
Email info@imaan.org.uk

Trades Union Congress
(LGB Trade Union Issues)
Congress House
Great Russell Street
London WC1B 3LS
Telephone 020 7636 4030
Email ppurton@tuc.org.uk

Stonewall Housing Association
(LGB housing and homelessness)
2a Leroy House
436 Essex Road
London N1 3QP
Telephone 020 7359 6242
Email info@stonewallhousing.org

National Gay Funeral Advice Helpline
Telephone 0800 281345

DISCUSSION OF QUESTIONNAIRE

Clarification and discussion about the questionnaire at the beginning of this text.

Having read some of the issues in this book, your reactions to the questions might be different from the ones you had initially and you may now be able to expand on your ideas. Perhaps you will discuss them further with other people.

1. Very few lesbians, gay men or bisexuals reveal their sexuality to all people. It is therefore unlikely that you will be aware of the numbers of gay people you have met. It is, however, highly likely that you have met many in your life without having recognised them.

2. It is impossible to be sure. The British government estimates between 5–7% (about one in fifteen). Stonewall, the campaign group for gay rights based in London, feels this is a reasonable guesstimate. However, many lesbians, gay men and bisexuals feel the percentage to be much higher.

3. To 'treat everyone the same' on the face of it seems a laudable concept – it sounds equitable. However, humankind is not identical. Each individual has different needs, different backgrounds/histories, religions, cultures, skin colours and, for our purposes, sexual orientations. All these differences should be taken into account when assessing 'need'. Understanding and accepting diversity is the key to good practice.

4. The issue of equal opportunities relates to the question we have discussed above. Dictionary definitions are short statements, such as: 'the opportunity or right to be employed, paid etc. without discrimination on grounds of sex, race etc.' (*Concise Oxford English Dictionary*). To attain any meaningful equality, however, the issue becomes more complex. A commitment to provide environments where people are not excluded from society would be needed; that is, an environment where diversity is embraced and catered for in every circumstance. This needs concerted planning, training and development; with positive action, not passive statements.

5. You have read in this book many issues relating to older gay people. You will have learnt that to be older and lesbian, bisexual or gay is still not easy. Many will have been subjected to discriminatory practices in their lives. Their histories have a poignancy that requires particular understanding. Care service providers need to be aware of individual special needs.

6. Lesbians, gay men or bisexuals rarely fit the general stereotypes encouraged by the media which are fuelled by prejudice and discrimination. Some are confident in their sexuality and like to conform to an agreed fashion or behaviour. However, most do not. Homosexual people span all ages, cultures, classes and creeds worldwide and fit into their particular societies just like anyone else.

7. Many older gay people have had children within a heterosexual relationship. In a society which is assumed to be heterosexual, the pressure is great to conform and many gay people find themselves accepting what is seen to be 'the norm' (the nuclear family) in their earlier years. Some gay couples decide to have children by IVF or other means; some adopt. Therefore, it cannot be assumed that everyone who has children is heterosexual.

8. Research has shown that a significant percentage of older homosexual people would prefer dedicated care services. Some gay people have little in common with heterosexuals. Others have socialised only with other lesbians or gay men throughout their lives, thus living in a distinct culture. Many have experienced devastating homophobia. The anxiety of potential prejudice and discrimination in old age is very real and clearly many would prefer to be cared for only in a gay environment.

9. Throughout society many of our social, economic, religious and educational institutions assume and promote the idea that heterosexuality is the norm - this is what is known as institutional homophobia. Internalised homophobia is a personal assimilation of established ideas from society; this can lead to internalised self-doubt and disgust.

10. Talking about sexual matters has long been a sensitive subject in our society. Many people, both heterosexual and homosexual, feel that sex is very much a personal thing and a private matter. However, while prejudice and institutional homophobia still exist, the personal becomes political. To eliminate discrimination against gay people, the issues of sexual orientation should remain in the wider public arena, while at same time assuring privacy in individual personal lives.

References

Adler, S.R., McGraw, S.A. and McKinley, J.B. (1998) Patient assertiveness in ethnically diverse older women with breast cancer: Challenging stereotypes of the elderly. *Journal of Aging Studies*, 12, 331–50.

Age Concern (2001) *'Opening Doors': Older Lesbian and Gay People – Forgotten No More*. London: Age Concern.

Age Concern (2001) *Opening Doors*. Research and Development Unit: Age Concern, England.

Age Concern (2001) *Opening Doors, Working with Older Lesbians and Gay Men*. Practice Guidance Resource Pack. Available from: www.ageconcern.org.uk/openingdoors (accessed 7 August 2007).

Age Concern (2007) *Definition of Ageism*. Available from: www.ageconcern.org.uk/AgeConcern/Ageism_about.asp (accessed May 2007).

Age Exchange. Intergenerational Arts and Learning Programme. Available from: www.age-exchange.org.uk (accessed 1 August 2007).

Andrews, M. (1999) The seductiveness of agelessness. *Ageing and Society*, 19 (3), 301–18.

Annison, J. (2000) Towards a clearer understanding of the meaning of home. *Journal of Intellectual Disability*, 25 (4), 251–62.

Arnstein, S.R. (1971) A ladder of citizen participation. *Journal of the Royal Town Planning Institute*, April, 1–6.

Audit Commission (2004) *Older People – Independence and Wellbeing: The Challenge for Public Services*. Audit Commission Publications.

Barnett, B. (2006) Feminist scholarship as a foundation for teaching about ageism in the academy. *NWSA Journal*, 18, 1 (Spring), 85–98.

Bauer, M., McAuliffe, L. and Nay, R. (2007) Sexuality, health care and the older person: an overview of the literature. *International Journal of Older People Nursing*, 2, 63–8.

Bayliss, K. (2000). Social work values, anti-discriminatory practice and working with older lesbian service users. *Social Work Education*, 19 (1), 45–53.

Ben-Ari, A.T. (2001) Homosexuality and heterosexism: views from academics in the helping professions. *British Journal of Social Work*, 31, 119–31.

Berkman, C.S. and Zinberg, G. (1997) Homophobia and heterosexism in social workers. *Social Work*, 42 (4), 319–32.

Biggs, S., Phillipson, C., Money, A. and Leach, R. (2006) The age-shift: observations on social policy, ageism and the dynamics of the adult lifecourse. *Journal of Social Work Practice*, 20 (3), 239–50.

Bourdieu, P. (1997) *Language and Symbolic Power*. Oxford: Blackwell Publishing.

Brown, H.C. (1998) *Social Work and Sexuality: Working with Lesbians and Gay Men*. London: Macmillan.

Butler, R.N. (1989) Dispelling ageism: the cross cutting intervention. *Annals of the American Academy of Social Science*, 503, 138–47.

Cabinet Office (2001) Social Exclusion Unit website. Available at: www.socialexclusionunit.gov.uk (accessed 4 September 2007.)

Carr, S. (2003) *Lesbian and gay perspectives on mental distress*, Presentation given at a Social Perspectives Network Study Day, Start Making Sense…Developing social models to understand and work with mental distress, 11 November 2002, pp. 33–36. Available from: www.spn.org.uk/fileadmin/SPN_uploads/Documents/Papers/ SPN_Papers/spn_paper_3.pdf (accessed 27 November 2007).

Carr, S.V., Scoular, A., Elliot, L., Llett, R. and Meager, M. (1999) A community-based lesbian sexual health service – clinically justified or politically correct? *Journal Family Planning* 25 (3), 93–5.

Census (2001) London: HMSO.

Centre for Policy on Ageing (1996) *A Better Home Life*. London: CPA.

Civil Partnership Act (2004). London: HMSO.

Codling, V. (2004) Cited in *BBC News 24*, 24 September 2006. Have the police overcome gay prejudice? By Tom Geoghegan *Online magazine*. http://news.bbc.co.uk/1/hi/magazine/3701218.stm

Cooper, C. (2003) *Out of the Past: Abseiling Dykes*. Available at: www.rainbownetwork.com/Features/ detail.asp?iData=14773&iCat=32&iChannel=25&nChannel=Features (accessed 12 June 2007).

Cree, W. and O'Corra, S. (2006) *Core Training Standards for Sexual Orientation: Making National Health Services Inclusive for LGB People*. London: Department of Health. Available from: www.dh.gov.uk/EqualityAndHumanRights (accessed 10 July 2007)

Department of Health (1989) *Homes Are For Living In*. London: HMSO.

Department of Health (1991) *Care Management and Assessment: Practitioners' Guide*. London: Department of Health.

Department of Health (1998) *Modernising Social Services: Promoting Independence, Improving Protection and Raising Standards* (CM4169). London: The Stationery Office.

Department of Health (2000) *A Quality Strategy for Social Care*. London: Department of Health.

Department of Health (2001) *The National Service Framework for Older People*. London: HMSO.

Department of Health (2002) *Requirements for Social Work Training*, Vol. 2004. General Social Care Council, London: HMSO.

Department of Health (2002) *Women's Mental Health: Into the Mainstream. Strategic Development of Mental Health Care for Women*. London: Department of Health.

Department of Health (2003) *Direct Payments Guidance: Community Care, Services for Carers and Children's Services (Direct Payments Guidance England 2003)*. London: Department of Health.

Department of Health (2004) *The National Service Framework for Older People*. London: Department of Health.

Department of Health (2006) *Core Training Standards for Sexual Orientation: Making Health Services Inclusive for Lesbian, Gay and Bisexual (LGB) People*. London: Department of Health.

Department of Health (2006a) *Core Training Standards for Sexual Orientation* (4.0.6). Available from: www.dh.gov.uk/EqualityAndHumanRights (accessed 10 July 2007).

Department of Health (2006b) *Real stories, real lives: LGBT people in the NHS, a modular resource produced by the Sexual Orientation and Gender Identity Strategy.* Available from: www.dh.gov.uk/EqualityAndHumanRights (accessed 10 July 2007).

Department of Social Security (2000) *Life Begins at 50.* London: Department of Social Security.

Department for Work and Pensions (2005) *Opportunity Age.* London: Department for Work and Pensions.

Depres, C. (1991) The meaning of home: literature review and directions for future research and theoretical development. *The Journal of Architectural and Planning Research*, 8 (2), 96–115.

Dorset LAGLO (2007) www.dorset.police.uk/default.aspx?page=375 (accessed June 2007).

Duberman, M. (1993) *Stonewall.* New York: Plume Press.

Dwyer, S. (2005) Older people and permanent care: Whose decision? *British Journal of Social Work*, 35, 1081–92.

Equality Act (2006). London: HMSO.

Equality Act (Sexual Orientation) Regulations (2007). London: HMSO.

Equality and Diversity: The Way Ahead (2006) London: HMSO. Government publication.

Federation for Community Development Learning (2002) *Sharing practice sheet 1.* Available from: www.fcdl.org.uk (accessed 17 July 2007).

Field, N. (1995) *Over the Rainbow – Money, Class and Homophobia.* London: Pluto Press.

Fish J. (2005) Lesbian and Health: UK National Lesbians and Health Care Survey. *Women and Health*, 41 (3), 27–45.

Foucault, M. (1980) *Power/Knowledge: Selected Interviews and Other Writings 1972–1977.* London: Harvester Press.

Gay and Grey in Dorset (2006) *Lifting the Lid on Sexuality and Ageing.* Bournemouth: Help and Care Development.

Gay-Glos. Available from: www.gay-glos.org (accessed 6 August 2007).

General Social Care Council (2002) *Codes of Practice for Social Care Workers and Employers.* Available from: www.gscc.org.uk (accessed 1 October 2007).

Gilliatt, S., Fenwick, J. and Alford, D. (2000) Public services and the consumer: empowerment or control? *Social Policy and Administration*, 34 (3), 333–49.

Gold, D. (2005) *Sexual exclusion issues and best practice in lesbian, gay and bisexual housing and homelessness.* Shelter/Stonewall Housing. Available from: www.casweb.org/stonewallhousing (accessed 21 November 2007).

Gorman-Murray, A. (2006) Gay and lesbian couples at home: identity work in domestic space. *Home Cultures*, 3 (2), 145–67.

Greater London Authority (2006) *Sexual Orientation Equality Scheme; 'From isolation to inclusion'.* London: Greater London Authority.

Hanley, B., Bradburn, J., Barnes, M., Evans, C., Goodare, H., Kelsom, M., Kent, A., Oliver, S., Thomas, S. and Wallcraft, J. (2004) *Involving the Public in NHS, Public Health and Social Care Research: Briefing notes for researchers* (second edition). INVOLVE.

Harris, B. (1997) *Ageing and Society*, 17 (5), September, 491–512.

Hartman, A. (1992) In search of subjugated knowledge. *Social Work*, 37 (6), 483–4.

Hayfield, A. (1995) 'Several faces of discrimination'. In V. Mason-John (Ed.) *Talking Black; Lesbians of African and Asian Descent Speak Out*. London: Cassell.

Healy, K. (2001) Participatory action research and social work: a critical appraisal. *International Social Work*, 44 (1), 93–105.

Heaphy, B. and Yip, A.K.T. (2006) Policy implications of ageing sexualities. *Social Policy and Society*, 5 (4), 443–51.

Heaphy, B., Yip, A.K.T. and Thompson, D. (2003) *Lesbian, Gay and Bi-sexual Lives over 50*. ESRC funded project report. Nottingham: The Nottingham Trent University, York House Publications.

Heaphy, B., Yip, A.K.T. and Thompson, D. (2004) Ageing in a non-heterosexual context. *Ageing and Society*, 24, 881–902.

Heaphy, B., Yip, A.K.T. and Thompson, D. (2004a) *Lesbian, Gay and Bisexual Lives over 50. A Report on the Project 'The Social and Policy Implications of Non-heterosexual Ageing*. Nottingham Trent University: York House Publications.

Heaphy, B., Yip, A. and Thompson, D. (2004b) Ageing in a non-heterosexual context. *Ageing and Society*, 24, 881–902.

Hefferman, K. (2006) Does language make a difference in health and social care practice? Exploring the new language of the service user in the United Kingdom. *International Social Work*, 49, 825–30.

Herdt, G., Beeler, J. and Rawls, T.W. (1997) Life course diversity among older lesbians and gay men: a study in Chicago. *Journal of Gay, Lesbian and Bi-sexual Identity*, 2 (3/4), 231–46.

Herek, G.M. (1991) 'Stigma, prejudice and violence against lesbians and gay men'. In J.C. Gonsiorek and J.D.Weinrech (Eds) *Homosexuality; Research Implications for Public Policy*. Newbury Park: Sage.

Heron, J. (1996) *Co-operative inquiry: research into the human condition*. London: Sage.

Higgins, A., Barker, P. and Begley, C.M. (2006) Sexuality: The challenge to espoused holistic care. *International Journal of Nursing Practice*, 12, 345–51.

Hinchliff, S., Gott, M. and Galena, E. (2004) 'I daresay I might find it embarrassing': General practitioners' perspectives on discussing sexual health issues with lesbian and gay patients. *Health and Social Care in the Community*, 13 (4), 345–53.

Hocking, J. (2006) *Advocacy and Older People*. Community Care special report. Available from: www.Communitycare.co.uk (accessed 7 August 2007).

Holah, M. and Davies, J. (2006) *Social Identity Theory*. Available from www.LearnPsychology.net (accessed 2 August 2007).

Home Office (2007) *Participating on equal terms. Equality and Diversity*. www.homeoffice.gov.uk/equalityanddiversity (accessed June 2007).

Hubbard, R. and Rossington, J. (1995) *As We Grow Older: A study of the housing and support needs of older lesbians and gay men*. London: Polari Housing Association.

Hughes, G. (2003) Talking about sexual identity with older men. *Australian Social Work*, 56 (3), 258–66.

Katz, S. (1996) *Disciplinary Old Age: The Formation of Gerontological Knowledge*. Charlottesville: University Press of Virginia.

King, M. and McKeown, E. (2003) *Mental Health and Social Wellbeing of Gay Men, Lesbians and Bisexuals in England and Wales*. London: MIND.

Kinsey, A. (1953) *Sexual Behaviour in the Human Female*. Philadelphia: Saunders.

Kinsey A., Pomeroy, W.B., Martin, C.E and Gebhard, P.H. (1948) *Sexual Behaviour in the Human Male*. Philadelphia: Saunders.

Knitting Circle (2001) *Pride History*. Available at: www.knittingcircle.org.uk/pridehistory.html (accessed June 2007).

Langley, J. (2001) Developing anti-oppressive empowering social work practice with older lesbian women and gay men. *British Journal of Social Work*, 31, 917–32.

Levenson, R. (2003) *Auditing Age Discrimination: A Practical Approach to Promoting Equality in Health and Social Care*. London: Kings Fund Publications.

Logan, J. and Kershaw, S. (1994) Heterosexism and social work, education: the invisible challenge. *Social Work Education*, 13 (3), 61–80.

Loretto, W., Duncan, C. and White, P. (2000) Ageism and employment: controversies, ambiguities and younger people's perceptions. *Ageing and Society*, 20, 279-302.

Lupnitz, D. (1992) Nothing in common but their first names: The case of Foucault and White. *Journal of Family Therapy*, 14, 281–4.

McAuliffe, L., Bauer, M. and Nay, R. (2007) Barriers to the expression of sexuality in the older person: the role of the health professional. *International Journal of Older People Nursing*, 2, 69–75.

McFarlane, L. (1998) *Diagnosis Homophobic: The Experiences of Lesbians, Gay Men and Bisexuals in the Mental Health Services*. PACE UK.

McGhee, D. (2005) *Intolerant Britain? Hate, Citizenship and Difference*. Maidenhead: Open University Press.

McGlone E. and Fitzgerald, F. (2004) *Perceptions of Ageism in Health and Social Services in Ireland*. National Council on Ageing and Older People .

Manthorpe, J. and Price, E. (2003) *Out of the Shadows*. Community Care special report. Available from: www.Communitycare.co.uk (accessed 31 July 2007).

Maslow, A. (1954) *Motivation and Personality*. New York: Harper Row.

Morrison, V.L. (1988) Observation and snowballing: useful tools for research into illicit drug use? *Social Pharmacology*, 2, 247–71.

National AIDS Trust (2007) www.nat.org.uk/stigma.And-Discrimination (accessed May 2007).

National Statistics Online. Available from www.statistics.gov.uk (accessed June 2007).

National Union of Teachers (NUT) (2004) *Supporting Lesbian, Gay, Bisexual and Transgender Students: An issue for every teacher* (guidance pamphlet). Available from: www.teachers.org.uk (accessed June 2007).

Neville, S. and Henrickson, M. (2006) Perceptions of lesbian, gay and bisexual people of primary healthcare services. *Issues and Innovation in Nursing Practice*, 55 (4), 407–15.

Places for People (1999) *Housing Needs of Older Lesbians and Gay Men in the North East*. Preston: Places for People.

Postle, K., Wright, P. and Beresford, P. (2005) Older people's participation in political activity – making their voices heard: a potential support role for welfare professional in countering ageism and social exclusion. *Practice*, 17 (3), 173–89.

Pugh, S. (2005) Assessing the cultural needs of older lesbians and gay men: implication for practice. *Practice: a Journal of the British Association of Social Workers*, 17 (3), 207–18.

River, L. (2006) *A Feasibility Study of the Needs of Older Lesbians in Camden and Surrounding Boroughs – a Report to Age Concern Camden*. London: Polari.

Rivers, I. (2004) Recollections of bullying at school and their long term implications for lesbians, gay men and bisexuals. *Crisis Volume*, 25 (4). *Hogrefe and Huber*.

Ross, F., Donovan, S., Brearley, S., Victor, C., Cottee, M., Crowther, P. and Clark, E. (2005) Involving older people in research: Methodological issues. *Health and Social Care in the Community*, 13 (3), 268–275

Savin-Baden, M. (2004) Achieving reflexivity: Moving researchers from analysis to interpretation in collaborative inquiry. *Journal of Social Work Practice*, 18 (3) 365–378.

Schaie, K.W. (1993) Ageist language in psychological research. *American Psychologist*, 48, 49-51.

Sexual Offences Act (1967). London: HMSO.

Sixsmith, J. (1986) The meaning of home: an exploratory study of environmental experience. *Journal of Environmental Psychology*, 6, 281–98.

Smale, G., Tuson, G. and Statham, D. (2000) *Social Work and Social Problems: Working Towards Social Inclusion and Social Change*. Basingstoke: Macmillan.

Smith, J. (2006) Quoted by University of Surrey, Human Resources Dept http://portal.surrey.ac.uk/portal/ page?_pageid =712,879005&_dad=portal&_schema=PORTAL (accessed 28 January 2008).

Smith, S.G. (1994) The essential qualities of a home. *Journal of Environmental Psychology*, 14, 31–46.

Southampton City Council (2007) *Working with Diversity and Discrimination* Handout. Training modular course.

Springfield, F. (2002) Lesbians, gays and transsexuals in care homes. *Nursing and Residential Care*, 4 (12), 586–88.

Stonewall (2007a) *Facts and figures.* www.stonewall.org.uk/education_for_all/research/1744.asp (accessed June 2007).

Stonewall (2007b) www.stonewall.org.uk (accessed June 2007).

Stonewall (2007c) www.stonewall.org.uk/information (accessed July 2007).

Stonewall (2007a) www.stonewall.org.uk/information_bank/health/default.asp (accessed 23 May 2007).

Stonewall (2007b) www.stonewall.org.uk/information_bank_/frequently_ asked_ questions/179.asp (accessed 23 May 2007).

Straker, D. (2002) *Cognitive Dissonance*. Available from: www.ChangingMinds.org [accessed: 31st July 2007].

Summerskill, C. (2007) *Gateway to Heaven*. DVD available from Age Concern: www.ageconcern.org.uk/openingdoors

Swantz, M. (1996) A personal position paper on participatory research: personal quest for living knowledge. *Qualitative Inquiry*, March, 2 (1), 120–37.

Tanner, D. (2003) Older people and access to care. *British Journal of Social Work*, 33, 499–515.

Tatchell, P. (1999) *Making a Scene*. Lecture given at a conference at the University of Central England. Available from: www.petertatchell.net/outrage/protestperformanc.htm (accessed June 2007).

Tegg, C. (2006) *Core Training Standards for Sexual Orientation. Making National Health Services Inclusive For LGB people*. www.dh.gov.uk/prod_consum_dh/idcplg?IdcService=GET_FILE&dID=20412&Rendition=Web

The Employment Equality *(Age) Regulations* 2006. London: HMSO.

Thompson, N. and Thompson, S. (2001) Empowering older people, beyond the care model. *Journal of Social Work*, 1 (1), 61–76.

Trotter, J. and Hafford-Letchfield, T. (2006) *Promoting Best Practice in Dealing with Sexual Orientation Issues*. Available from: www.communitycare.co.uk (accessed 16 March 2007).

Troyna, B. and Carrington, B. (1989) 'Whose side are we on?' Ethical dilemmas in research on 'race' and 'education'. In R. G. Burgess (ed.) *The Ethics of Educational Research*. Lewes: Falmer.

Turner, W.J. (1995) Homosexuality, type 1: an Xg 28 phenomenon. *Archives of Sexual Behaviour*, 2, 109–134.

Waitt, G., and Gorman-Murray, A. (2007). Provincial paradoxes: 'at home' with older gay men in a provincial town of the Antipodes. In *Queer Space: Centres and peripheries, 21 February*. Sydney, University of Technology, 1–6..

Warwick, I., Chase, E. and Aggleton, P. (2004) *Homophobia, Sexual Orientation and Schools: A Review and Implication for Action*. London: London University.

Weeks, J. (1989) *Sex, Politics and Society*. London: Longman.

Williamson, I. (2000) Internalized homophobia and health issues affecting lesbians and gay men. *Health Education Research* 15(1), 97–107.

Wilson, C. (2007) LGBT politics and sexual liberation. *International Socialism*, Issue 114, 137–66. Available from: www.isj.org.uk (accessed 24 April 2007).

Index

95